PLEASE REGISTER MY OWNERSHIP OF
COWBOY POETRY CONTEMPORARY VERSE BY *Duke Davis*

I HAVE COPY NUMBER _____ 0699 _____

NAME _____

ADDRESS _____

CITY _____ STATE _____ ZIP _____

COWBOY MINER PRODUCTIONS
PO BOX 9674
PHOENIX, AZ 85068

Collector's edition

2,000 numbered registered copies

This copy is number <u>0699</u>

Cowboy Poetry

Contemporary Verse
by Duke Davis

Foreword by
Warren Miller

Illustrated by Ron Kil

Edited by Janice and Mason Coggin

Cowboy Miner
PRODUCTIONS

Cowboy Poetry, Contemporary Verse by Duke Davis
Copyright 2000 Duke and Ruth Davis
Illustrations Copyright 2000 by Ron Kil
Edited by Janice and Mason Coggin
Publisher:
      Cowboy Miner Publications
      P.O. Box 9674
      Phoenix, AZ 85068
      Phone: (602)944-3763
      Cowboypros@aol.com

Publisher's Cataloging in Publication Data

Davis, Duke 1947–
Cowboy Poetry Contemporary Verse by Duke Davis/
    Duke Davis. Edited by Janice and Mason Coggin.
    Foreword by Warren Miller.
      p. cm.

ISBN 0-9662091-4-1

1. Cowboy—Poetry. 2. Ranch Life—Poetry and Prose. 3. West
    (US)—Poetry and Prose.
    I.   Title
    Library of Congress Catalog Card Number: 00-103499

Book design & Typesetting: SageBrush Publications , Tempe, AZ
Jacket Design: ATG Publications, Phoenix, AZ
Printing: Bang Printing, Brainerd, MN
Printed and bound in the United States of America

Acknowledgements

Many thanks to all the fine ranches I've had the pleasure of working on or visiting, including the Bar S Bar Ranch, Dry Creek Ranch, Amber Rose Ranch, Horse Prairie Ranch, Deseret Land & Livestock, McNeil Ranch, Horn Five Ranch, TX Ranch, Fulton Ranch and Buckhorn Ranch. My saddle time at these ranches provided the inspiration and opportunity to write most of this text.

To my good friends who are all great cowboys: Tuffy Cooper, Red Steagall, Waddie Mitchell, Larry McWhorter, Gary Morton, Mackey Hedges, Les Buffham, Paige McNeil, Carson Scheller, Bill King amd Lynn Sims. Thanks pards, for ridin' point.

A very special thanks to Mason and Janice Coggin for not only encouraging me, but for editing and assembling this body of work, and to Warren Miller and the Sharlot Hall Museum in Prescott, Arizona, for their friendship and support.

To my friend, Ron Kil, *muchas gracias, amigo.* Your excellent illustrations are more than a contribution to this book . . . they are the book!

Most of all, to my dear wife, Ruthie, whose strength never waivers, I will love and cherish you for eternity.

"I've never laid claim to be much of a cowboy, but I've dang shore rode with more'n a few."

Duke Davis

Dedication

This body of work is dedicated to my Lord and Savior, Jesus Christ, who makes all things possible. All grace and glory go to Him.

Contents

Foreword

This is a book about friendship. Which will come as no surprise to anyone who knows Duke and Ruthie Davis, two of the most genuinely friendly people you could ever meet. This is a book full of friends and mentors and kinship and respect, full of honest treatment.

Some of the friends are cohorts, fellow riders of the canyons and ridges, grasslands and tall timber, mountains and meadows. Duke is most at home with brush country cowboys kicking leppys out of thickets, respected teachers with insight into how to think like a horse or turn a phrase like a philosopher. Some critters who have shared his life are a few good dogs, a very few good horses, a Green Mojave rattlesnake.

Duke ranges far and wide in his choice of stories, drawing from Mari Sandoz, from handwritten diaries in the archives of the Autrey Museum, from tales told by bunkhouse friends. Some involve names we all consider friends: William S. Hart, Charlie Russell. Most are the plain folk we are glad to meet through Duke's tales because they are good and honest and true.

Duke's poetry is richly reminiscent of the classics of cowboy verse, and realized with such facility that the verse doesn't intrude on the telling of the stories. Lean back and hang on for an enjoyable ride through a world where the stench of burning hide and hair mingles with mountain honeysuckle, where cowdogs can not only ear-tag heifers, but a really good one can call you on the phone to tell you he has finished. Meet an uncle who only became a world traveler after being nailed snugly into his coffin, and a horse trainer whose singing is worse than any quirt.

Duke gives us sage advice that, one suspects, he had to learn the hard way: beware of company saddles, lady-broke horses; never argue with a cook, a mule, or a skunk! Here are the stories that are Duke, whose cowboy heart, as he says of his mentor Buck Ramsey, is tied hard and fast.

Warren Miller
Prescott Arizona
March, 2000

One Good Dog

When I was a sprout growin' up, my grandpa said to me,
"The best things you acquire in life are mostly always free."

At the moment I understood that only time would tell,
but, now that I'm grown, I figger I learned his lesson well.

You see, if you can count your friends on the fingers of just one hand,
then you've led a life that's full and rich, and you're a lucky man.

You might ride three good horses for every hundred head,
and maybe know two good women before you're laid down dead
But, the one thing I remember and I've understood throughout,
with all the things a man could have and learn to live without…

was made so clear to me in the old man's clever dialogue,
it's the value..and trust…and friendship of ownin' just one good dog!

Well, there's heelers, and hunters, and little cute ones for a show,
there's fighters, and swimmers,
and some pedigrees that I don't even know.

Now, my dog ain't got no papers, he's just a mixed breed mutt,
but, he's a right handy little booger when I got cows to cut.

He'll cull the yearlin' bulls and turn 'em in the pen,
then look around at me just hopin' we can play that little game again!

He don't chase the chickens, or nip at horses feet;
he'll work through the icy winter and the blasted summer heat.

I can take him fishin', and he'll just lay there real polite,
until my line's a-jerkin' and I got myself a bite.

And when we're out deer huntin' I'll draw a bead and aim,
he'll freeze…and hold his breath…so's not to scare the game.

And when the neighbors are over for a down-home Bar-B-Q,
he'll sit and mind his manners till you pass him a bone to chew.

And with kids, well, he's number one, he just loves to run and play;
he'll play tag forever chasin' youngin's through the hay.

I can throw him in the pickup when it's rainin' hard outside,
but, he'd justa soon jog in the mud than to hop on for a ride!

He's never in a hurry, but I've never had to wait,
I just stay behind the wheel of the truck,
'cause now he's learned to work a gate!

He makes a right fine hand, and as a friend he's the very best;
he don't ever even argue, or make hisself a pest!

He'll do the work of two good men, and whatever else I might need,
he gratefully accepts the task, and he's dang shore cheap to feed!

And when the day is over, he'll put his head down on my lap,
and give me that loyal stare before he fades off into a nap.

Now, every dog I've ever owned had a barn in which to reside,
but, this one, well, he's kinda special, so he sleeps with me inside.

There's many a fool I know that I owe no apology,
to say a dog is just a dog, why, that's just bovine scrapology!

Yes, he is man's best friend, and what a befitting epilogue,
and I know the value…and trust…
and friendship, of ownin' just one good dog.

A lot of folks who are "anti" dog will never understand
that they're more than just tools to work stock with. Like
horses, the good ones are rare, but when you find one, they
become like family.

Stare into the Fire

There's somethin' 'bout starin' into a fire
    that makes a soul quite serene.
    It seems to unfold forgotten memories,
    as it makes your mind sharp and keen.

It's a good time to remember…or forget…
    whatever the case might be,
    and it gives you a chance to work through things
    when you're too blinded to see.

Any youngster can sit and stare at it,
    and his attention will never stray,
    as the vision of his future comes alive,
    with a flaming log to light the way.

It's impossible not to feel the safety and warmth,
    as the flames leap and dance,
    drawing a picture for the observer
    that lures you into a hypnotic trance.

If you're a little older, it's different,
    a fleeting chance to reflect,
    seeking clues in the here and now
    that only hot burning coals can detect.

Every familiar emotion can be found
    as you watch it brightly glow,
    exploring forgotten corners of your mind,
    looking for answers you don't know.

You can recall your first sweetheart…
   love lost…and forlorn
   or remember that cold, rainy night
   when your oldest child was born.

It's a time to make your plans,
   or ponder on the drought;
   try to figger ways to cut a corner,
   on what you can live without.

It's a perfect opportunity
   to appreciate your wife,
   and thank the Good Lord above
   for blessin' you with such a good life.

But, the old-timer derives the most
   from sittin' in front of a fire.
   For you see…their life is almost over,
   and soon they will expire.

They've seen it all, and had their life's dreams
   some are good and some are bad;
   but, they seem to have it all in perspective,
   whether they're happy or they're sad.

So, next time you see your elder
   gazin' into the embers,
   kindly keep your silence,
   and just try to remember…

That they've earned their place in life,
   for that you should admire,
   and their kindlin' is all used up,
   with the last of their desire.

Finally, the day will come
    when your flames turn to ash,
    then, you're the old-timer...
    and your life before you will flash.

Come your judgement day,
    ye reap what ye shall sow,
    and God will count the tally,
    when your time has come to go.

So, if you live your life correctly,
    you'll have what you require,
    respect...and peace of mind...
    before you burn your very last fire.

    Fires are timeless. Most of us are fascinated by a campfire our whole life. A person can really get lost in their thoughts starin' at one, and it seems the older you get, the more treasures they hold for you.

Bernice and the Singin' Horse Trainer

Down behind Bernice's horse ranch
    in this little ol' shack,
buried underneath old saddles, a pile a-ropes
    and weathered old tack,
lives my best friend
    whose name it's best I just leave out,
but some of ya-ll will know
    exactly who I'm talkin' about.

Now, Bernice trains
    some of the best endurance horses around,
all stouthearted hot bloods
    that are fast, solid and sound.
Her methods sure work
    'cause there's awards coverin' her walls;
trophies adorn her tack room
    and ribbons are hangin' above the stalls.

I inquired one day,
    "Bernice, how do you build such a handle on a horse?
I'd like to know your secret,
    and others would, too, of course."
She tells me,
    "It's really quite simple to win enduros with a ringer,
and I owe it all to your friend
    who fashions himself to be a good singer."

"You see, your ol ' pard's tone deaf
    and can't even carry a tune,
but his howlin' helps me train my horses
    whenever he tries to croon.
I take him with me
    when I start leggin' my colts out on the trail,
and politely request a song,
    and he obligingly starts to wail."

"He breaks into 'Little Joe The Wrangler'
    and that colt hits a trot,
that's 'bout a 4-inute ditty,
    so it gets 'em loose and kinda hot.
Then he goes into 'Streets Of Laredo'
    and they shift into a lope,
that pony starts a-runnin'
    like he's juiced up on dope."

"But, then comes the clincher
    when he sings 'Ghost Riders In The Sky';
that horse will split the breeze
    and really start to fly.
Now, how I keep 'em at that gait
    I fear I'm as guilty of this lurid crime,
if he stops a-singin' I holler….
    LET'S HEAR IT ONE MORE TIME!"

Well, this satisfied my curiosity
    of how she trained a horse so well,
great conformation on her animals
    and they all can run like Hell!
But, then the thought hit me
    and I asked her without jest,
"I reckon his singin' sparks 'em alright…
    but, when do they ever rest?"

She says, "That's easy, I put 'em in the corral
    and throw 'em a flake.
Then he starts recitin' poetry,
    and that's a boredom no horse can take.
So, they're exercised and fed,
    and all a-restin' in their pen,
then we get up the next day...
    and do it all over again!"

I know his voice ain't purty,
    but is it really all that bad?
Bernice says, "You bet it is...but
    he's still the best dang trainer I've ever had!"
She said when she's buried
    and 'oer her grave her friends will weep,
she's gonna have him sing at her funeral...
    "'CAUSE THAT VOICE WOULD RAISE THE DEAD FROM
    THEIR SLEEP!"

                        ❧   ☙

    It's no secret any more who this is about. It's Les
Buffham, famed yuppie cowboy poet. One day, when he
first started to work singin' into his act, I rode down in the
canyon where he was livin' and heard the most gawd awful
howlin' comin' from his ol' trailer and the durn thing was
rockin' back and forth! Bernice does raise some fine
endurance horses, but I'll guarantee you, his singin' has
little to do with her success!

Six Whistle Blows

The other mornin' I awoke from a peaceful sleep,
    with a sound of a lonesome train whistle blowin'.
Even though I was emerged in a slumber so deep,
    I wondered where that ol' train was a-goin.

The first blast was so faint, signaling arrival,
    as it beckoned to my vagabond heart.
It stirred my youthful emotion of survival,
    that this was my last chance to depart.

I remembered a time long ago, when I first left home,
    leavin' that Texas town to wander,
and how I'd spent twenty years on the roam,
    as my life unfolded each memory grew fonder.

The second blast sharply cut through the air,
    with a sense of urgency that was foreboding.
Subconsciously, I spouted details lying dormant there,
    as I relived things time was eroding.

Bittersweet flashes came in opposite waves so clearly,
    things I'd done well but never succeeded;
an empty heart from a love I'd held so dearly;
    obstacles in life where progress was impeded.

The third blast filled up the early mornin' light,
    sending a message that I couldn't ignore.
It called out for action, like a bird in flight,
    or a suckling colt that was craving for more.

My sleepy mind responded with deep satisfaction,
    but of what there was, a mere hint of suggestion.
Everything came at once; I grabbed only a fraction.
    I knew the answer, but couldn't understand the question.

The fourth blast surrounded me and calmly I froze,
    suspended in time for what seemed to be an hour.
Engulfed in serenity I continued to doze,
    embraced by some hypnotic alien power.

A mixture of present and future resolve,
    I knew what was done would never change.
Then the sound of that whistle began to dissolve,
    and my fate I could never rearrange.

The fifth blast slowly faded echoing in my head,
    planting a seed for my life destination.
Suddenly, I could see all the world from my bed,
    as I had some sort of revelation.

My eyes never opened, caught in this dream,
    as my mind whirled in a haze,
seduced by a feelin' I was part of a team,
    of myself, and someone else's better days.

The sixth blast was final and could barely be heard,
    I held my breath for the final encore.
It was then I was delivered one parting wise word,
    and I knew what this drama was for.

It was the sound of my Grandpa's soft soothing voice,
    and my recollection of all he had told.
Then, magically I was transformed without any choice,
    and the words became my own, when I was old.

Is it an ageless dream, or does it just come in time;
    is it something that only God knows?
How could I be given memories, puzzles and rhymes,
    and live my life in six whistle blows?

ও ৎ

I sure did love my grandpa and I miss him a lot. It's funny how things like this dream can happen, kinda like our departed loved ones are sending us messages.

Buck Ramsey

He rode out one mornin',
    to rope and ride tall in the saddle,
    leather creakin' , to trot and trot again,
    with horses, men and cattle.

He responded to life
    and divine circumstance befalling;
    the earth, his mother, bade to him,
    and he answered her calling.

He became our mentor,
    linking present resolve to historic past;
    speaking our minds,
    his pulsating cowboy heart tied hard and fast.

What a vicarious existence we live
    through his persona and word,
    provoked by a lilting melody
    from his cow camp song we heard.

Only to find a hidden corner
    within our own troubled heart,
    where his kindred spirit gave comfort to us,
    never more to impart.

Did we become him, or he us,
    through a psychic healer's fever?
    How did we all transcend
    into the mind of Billy Deaver?

Oh, he's got the bark on,
    rough hewn as a trapper, but kindly gentle;
    a little playful at times,
    and more than slightly sentimental.

But, we feel we know him so well
    or is it hardly at all
    for he's become an icon to the West,
    a classic figure, grand and tall.

Yeah, he's put the feed bag on
    with presidents, professors and kings,
    but, deep within his puncher's heart
    the song of the prairie sings.

For he's a cowboy,
    no matter his gifts of the gab, or crafting verse and song,
    come first light of morn
    he'll be there, jinglin' the remuda along.

We hear his rowels ringin'
    and the echo of his lathered pony's trot,
    traversing the canyons of our mind,
    as we drink from his coffeepot.

So, when all's said and done,
    he'll be there, always by our side,
    whether it be 'round the campfire
    or beyond the Great Divide.

He'll do to ride the river with,
    and his legacy will never expire,
    may his camps always be dry
    and his horses sound, and stay out of the wire.

And when our numbered days on earth
   have reached their glorious end,
   may we all be ridin' for Ol' Buck's brand,
   to trot and trot again.

❦   ❧

    Buck Ramsey had more people genuinely love him than any man I've ever known. A few years before his passing, I was privileged to be a part of a tribute to him held in Amarillo, and I got to do this poem for him. I spent time with Buck in his living room pickin' and laughing, and he was always a constant source of inspiration and joy to my wife and me both. His funeral is something that will never be forgotten by those who were present. *Vaya con Dios,* Buck.

One More Wreck

I was day workin' the TX Ranch one spring,
    doin' a gather down Carlsbad way,
bringin' in calves for the first brandin',
    just a happy cowboy on a beautiful day.

My pony steps in a sand bog and swallers his head,
    sorta left me in a bad situation.
I flies clean outta my leather, but still got my reins,
    figgerin' I's 'bout to acquire some additional education!

Well, we goes to scramblin' in the sand together,
    both of us tryin' to recover from the wreck.
That colt's jes' tryin' to find some solid ground,
    and I'm buried plumb up to my neck!

We flopped and we floundered, and flailed all about,
    for what musta been nigh on an hour.
By the time that ol' hoss and I recovered our senses,
    we both looked like we's dunked in flour!

There was sand down my shirt, sand in my boots,
    a pound of it filled every pocket.
The colt ate his share, makin' my trip back to the ranch
    sorta like ridin' a runaway rocket!

I slides to a stop at the sortin' pens,
    and the boss says, "Where's your jag a-cows?"
Gamely I replied, "Saw a few ... here and there ...
    but I ain't got none," I allows.

"'Cause you see boss, I got kinda busy with my priorities,
    and I figger I'm smarter than any fox!
I thought to myself ... Now, wouldn't it be nice
    to bring this sand back and build your kids a sand box!"

Well, the boys shore got a snicker on my account,
    and the boss even laughed, by heck.
But, I had to circle back for them cows to save my job,
    but to me ... it was just one more wreck!

Destination Unknown

Last summer Ol' Uncle Clay died,
    and left Aunt Martha feelin' quite sad.
She called up Clay's brother, Harlen, and told him,
    "He wanted to be buried next to Dad."

Harlen says, "The ol' place was sold some twenty years ago,
    and I don't think they'd want him there.
Let's send him down to Texas to Sister Thelma;
    ship the box to me and I'll pay the fare."

So, Uncle Harlen sent him to Aunt Thelma,
    but she commenced to hit the roof.
"I don't want the sorry guzzler buried here," she says.
    "He was always drunk, and lazy, and aloof!"

So, she sent the box up to Cousin Henry,
    who had a farm up Oklahoma way.
He said, "It'll be a cold day in hell 'fore I bury him,
    he still owes me for six tons of hay!"

Henry forwarded the box to a relative I didn't even know,
    just a little north of Old Fort Union;
a second cousin, twice removed, on his brother's side,
    he'd met at some family reunion.

He didn't even know Uncle Clay,
    and contacted the government who just might know.
By October the box was a-headin' south
    to a coffee plantation in Puerto Rico!

We all lost track of Uncle Clay for a while,
    until we got a card at Christmas time.
Seems he ended up somewhere in Scotland
    with a sheepherder who didn't mind.

The card said, "I buried your poor ol' uncle
    'neath a tall and glorious tree.
Didn't know the lad, as you well know,
    but I'm hopin' you'd do the same for me."

"I didn't know what to put on his gravestone,
    but, Oh, what a beautiful stone I bought!
Engraved with ... 'Here lies someone's dear ol' uncle ...
    who sure traveled the world a lot!'"

Ridin' the Alley

I'll tackle any chore and with a smile what's more,
    'cause my handle's 'day workin' cowboy for hire'.
I might fix windmills, then doctor sick cattle ills,
    or dig postholes and run fence line wire.

I can twist a wrench, and haul hay in a pinch,
    or even muck horse stalls, putrid concoction.
But there ain't nothin' worse that'll get me to curse,
    than ridin' the alley at the sale barn auction!

It ain't the long hours, or the calves with the scours,
    and I don't even mind the blasted heat or the cold.
But, between you and me, it's dang hard to see,
    how any of that sorry stock ever gets sold!

There's a three-legged mule, who's startin' to drool,
    and a mustang colt with bangs and no ears.
We unload a Hereford dry, who's sportin' pink eye,
    buried 'neath two Corriente steers!

There's a burro that's blind, and a truckload of swine,
    two geese, and a crippled up deer.
Some old lady's cryin', as her milk cow is dyin',
    she's sayin', "Come on precious … Step on down here."

Finally, we unload the cattle and climb into the saddle,
    as the auctioneer starts a-barkin' the tally.
The yard boss calls the pen, then all the fun begins
    as cows come a-flyin' down the alley!

"310!" he yells. Oh, what the hell,
    I knew I shouldn'ta brought a green colt!
He's a-startin' to buck and I'm prayin' for luck,
    "NOT IN 312 YOU FEATHERHEAD DOLT!"

I finally get him on track, but he's got a hump in his back;
    I shore picked a heck of a time to do some horse trainin'!
"240!" the boss shouts, "and you fellas look out,
    pull your slickers off 'cause now it's a-rainin'."

I cut a corner too close, and the fence sends a dose
    of pain that seers from my kneecap to my head.
I'll see the doc in the mornin' and I'm sure I'll get a warnin'
    of how, if I'm not careful, I'll wind up dead!

Mosta the stock's been sold, 'cept what's quarantined or old,
    and my slicker's got a hole and I'm soaked.
When it rains it pours, and just when I think I can't take no more…
    OH NO, THAT OL' MILK COW JUST CROAKED!

The cows have been penned, and I'm a-hopin' I mend,
    after fifteen long hours in the saddle.
The trucks start to load, and pull off down the road,
    as we continue this bovine shippin' battle!

It's 2:00 in the mornin', and without any warnin',
    this brockleface bull goes on the hook!
He horns my ol' hoss, the crew and the boss,
    NOW, THEM RULES AIN'T WROTE IN NO BOOK!

Finally, the shippin's all through and we take in the view,
    surveyin' just what couldn't be sold.
There's the crippled ol' deer, the mustang with no ears,
    and the blind burro who's just too durned old!

The boss cuts my check, and you can bet, by heck,
    at ridin' the alley I'm all through!
No more of this mess, the pain and the stress,
    unless there ain't no other day work to do!

                 *   *

    Actually, I've always enjoyed workin' the sale barn in Lovington, New Mexico. Not real glamorous cowboy work, but it's a good crew, and an endless source of non-stop entertainment.

Sonny and His Stock Dog

I guess there's been a lot written 'bout stock dogs,
    their worth and how they work so well.
But, I'm gonna relate a little story that beats 'em all,
    that took place in San Angelo at the Cactus Hotel.

It seems that all the boys were sittin' 'round the lobby
    drinkin' beer, swappin' tales and boastin',
'bout who had the best dog to work sheep and cattle,
    and to each braggart's lie they were a-toastin'.

Now, braggin' in that part of Texas
    has been refined to a gentleman's game of art.
But, it seems no one could ever top ol' Sonny Nolke
    once he got his chance to start.

You see, ol' Sonny had mastered 'one-upsmanship'
    and he'd just wait till everyone was through.
Then he'd cut loose a real zinger
    that would top anything you could ever do.

Anyway, ol' Jim's a-braggin' on his blue heeler
    and how he could work a section with 500 head.
He said him and his ol' dog would have 'em penned and loaded
    long before lunch had been fed!

J.P. said that weren't nothin' to brag on,
    him and his ol' kelpie could match that feat.
Plus, his dog could cull out all the first year heifers
    and tag the ears before it was time to eat!

Well, it was getting' purty thick and deep
    when the phone rang off the wall,
and the barkeep yells over all the braggin',
    "Hey Sonny, ... you got a phone call!"

The boys just kept stackin' it higher and higher,
    and it had gone 'bout as far as it could go,
when Sonny hung up the phone and calmly returned
    to deliver his final blow.

We all turned to him and inquired, ...
    "Who was that on the line?"
Sonny just smiled, and quietly replied,
    "Oh, it was just that durn stock dog a-mine."

"He said he hated to call me here
    and you fellas know he seldom does...
but he'd just penned some sickly yearlin's
    and wanted to know where the terramycin was!"

Now, we all figgered Sonny sure won that round.
    I mean, after THAT what could a dog be expected to do?
So, we conceded he had the top dog,
    but how much he was sayin' we didn't know was true.

So it goes with braggarts and canines,
    but Sonny's final words were shocking indeed.
He said, "That terramycin was right next to the bag balm...
    I reckon I'm gonna have to teach that dumb mutt to read!"

❧ ❧

The late Sonny Nolke was well known in Texas and New Mexico in the ranching community, and his son, Monte, still writes for the *Livestock Journal*. This story is true in the sense that Sonny actually told it, but whether or not it was true, well, I'll let you decide for yourself.

The Hat Band

Livin' in the hill country of Texas,
    there's one thing that it takes,
and that's ... no fear in the fact
    you have to live with all them blasted rattlesnakes!

When I's growin' up, I learned to deal with 'em,
    and even went on a snake hunt now and then.
Shoot, I've made more'n one hat band
    from one I took a shovel to in the catch pen.

Now, you kill what you can, and live with the rest,
    but they're just Western Diamondbacks.
Out in California it's a little different
    when a Green Mojave snake crosses your tracks.

'Cause them Green Mojave's are more aggressive,
    a little smaller with a deadlier strike.
So, in the desert afternoon there ain't no such thing
    as a pleasure ride or a leisurely little hike!

So, one day I'm makin' my circle
    just as happy as could be,
when not more'n ten feet ahead in the trail,
    what the Hell do you think I'd see?

Yep ... that ol' snake's a-stretched out and a-sunnin'
    just straighter than a clothesline.
I figgered that ol' skin look real purty on my John B.
    so, Mr. Rattler ... I believe you're mine!

Now, I'd done this a time or two,
    so I knew to stay on my horse a-straddle.
I reached down and got my buck knife
    that I kept in a sheath on the near side of my saddle.

Feelin' like Jim Bowie ... I let 'er fly,
    hopin' to bury the blade deep in it's head.
But, as only my luck would have it,
    I hit it with the blunt end of the handle instead!

Even though I'd missed a clean kill,
    I did succeed in knockin' the poor thing senseless.
So ... I figgered I'd just take a boot to it,
    after all, it was dazed and defenseless!

I dismounted and looked for a rock
    like a warrior preparin' for battle.
When much to my dismay ...
    the damn thing started to rattle!

My adrenaline was a-pumpin' furiously,
    as I circled my victim, my prey.
Then I tripped over a gopher hole
    the fool varmint had put right there in my way!

My arms and legs went a-flyin'
    as I crashed and landed face down.
Naturally, this spooked my horse,
    so he's a-risin' high and homeward bound!

Now, Mr. Snake and I both lay there knocked plumb silly,
    just the two of us a-stretched out in the trail.
Each of us waitin' for the other to make his move,
    and the whole time he's a-waggin' that ol' tail!

We're nose to nose ... and frozen
    both with a fixed look in our eye,
knowin' that if either of us moved ...
    the other one's bound to die!

I reckon I musta hypnotized him,
    or he put me in a trance really deep.
I don't rightly know what happened,
    but I'll be danged if we both didn't go fast asleep!

Meanwhile, back at the ranch, Les spots my horse
    a-trottin' home on the double.
So he sets off to cover my tracks,
    figgerin' I must be in some sort of trouble.

He rides up and spots me and the reptile,
    motionless, and head-to-head.
I reckon the thought musta crossed his mind
    that possibly ... both of us were dead!

Ol' Les flies offa his horse ...
    runs up to check the lifeless bodies he's found.
He gave me and that ol' snake quite a scare,
    'cause we're both sound asleep there on the ground!

Mr. Rattler startles first,
    and Ol' Les jumps back to head south,
when I woke up with a mighty jolt
    and kicked the false teeth right outta his mouth!

Them ol' choppers flew through the air
    and bit the head clean offa that snake!
And a-course that started us to jawin'
    'bout what a fine hat band that skin would make.

Now, since it was his teeth that'd made the kill,
    Ol' Les wanted the skin that almost sealed my fate.
But I says, "Sorry, ol' pard, it's mine …
    'cause, after all … I's the one who had the bait!"

Another shot at my friend Les Buffham. We had some wonderful times ridin' the canyons of Santa Clarita Valley in California, and even encountered a snake or two. But I figger this certainly isn't any worse than some of the "windys" he's told!

The Broken Saddle

Gather 'round boys, stop all yer noise,
    get down from a-punchin' yer cattle.
This story begins, just like it ends,
    a saga of one broken saddle.

'Twas two years ago, I want you to know,
    while brandin' on Bar S Bar range,
that I first threw this kack on a company horse back,
    but the fit wasn't right, it was strange.

I's tied hard and fast, and my loop I did cast,
    at one deacon stray I'd found.
When the saddle, she blows, and a-sailin' I goes
    sorta pegged me head first in the ground!

The saddle was broke, that weren't no joke,
    it'd been down hard, dusty trails.
But the boss says, "I'll fix this seat with some tricks,"
    so, he drove in three one-inch nails.

I says to Ol' Jake, "Now, that's one big mistake;
    that patch job will surely not hold!"
But, the boss hit a lick, and hollers, "Resaddle quick!"
    So, I pushed on just like I's told.

Well, I's a-workin' the steers, early last year,
    on the Elliott Ranch up Visalia way.
I brought just one horse, but needed two a-course,
    so, from the remuda they roped me this ol' bay.

She was the last of the pickin's, and fulla the dickens;
    but, boys I'll ride anything with hair.
Broncy from winter, she looked like a sprinter,
    but, Hell, I didn't care.

I threw my weathered ol' kack astride her ol' back,
    and goes to strap 'er down real tight.
When my latigo breaks, "Not now for God's sake!"
    I'll be workin' cattle till late in the night.

I tried a twist and a braid, and every trick of the trade,
    when the boss barks, "WE AIN'T GONNA WAIT NO MORE!"
So, I went to the wagon, and commenced to draggin'
    out that company saddle from one year before.

I cinched 'er down tight, with alla my might,
    then on her back I did straddle.
I forked this raspy bay mare, who wasn't all there,
    perched in a time-bomb saddle.

Well, it shore didn't take long for the mare to go wrong,
    and my knees started turnin' to jelly.
'Cause the rig that I trusted ... once again had been busted,
    and the whole durn thing went under her belly.

Now, I'll ride with the best, and meet any test;
    however, I prefer to be the one on top.
But I was splittin' the breeze between the ol' bays knees,
    and figgered it was about time I should drop!

Well, drop's what I did, and I hit with a skid,
    preparin' to deal with my blunder.
She peppered my hide, and never broke stride,
    just hell-bent and kickin' like thunder!

She bucked and she spun, then broke to a run,
    with three cowboys glued to her tail.
They all joined the race, in a runaway chase,
    but ... I's laid out flat in the trail!

To all our surprise, she shot over the rise,
    drawin' a bead on the wagon.
Wall-eyed and screamin', like the devil's own demon,
    and that saddle she STILL was a-draggin'!

She sailed through the air, missed me by a hair,
    with all that riggin' a-floggin'.
The blankets were poppin'; she weren't ready fer stoppin';
    and them stirrups caught me right upside the noggin'!

I knew I's in trouble, and I started seein' double;
    boys, I's just plumb dizzy in the head.
I figgered I'd survive, and I knew I's alive,
    but, I also knew I's half dead!

The ropes were a-hissin', as the loops were a-missin',
    as them punchers were tryin' to rope the ol' bay.
I's kicked hard and tossed, my eyes were both crossed,
    and I's jes tryin' to get the Hell outta the way!

I's somewhat concerned, 'cause whenever I turned,
    that mare had me right in her sights.
I expected the worse, and continued to curse,
    'cause she had me nailed dead to rights!

The circle was tightened, and the ol' bay was shore frightened,
    as the boys were a-hollerin' all their advice.
The rig must be cut from the ol' mare's gut,
    and I knew I'd dang shore pay the price!

They squeezed her in tight, and continued the fight,
    as I waded through horse hooves a-stompin'.
My job was to drag the kack off that nag,
    who was crow-hoppin' high and rompin'!

Well, I cut the cinch from the wretched ol' wench,
    and how that ol' saddle was tattered.
The mare was all there, no worse for the wear,
    but, I's bruised, bloody and battered!

I lost a week's pay, in my bedroll I lay,
    Jes' a-waitin' to come to my senses.
I's prayin' to ride, some ol' mustang's hide.
    Hell, I wished I could even go mend some fences!

Well, I lived through that wreck, without breakin' my neck,
    though it took me quite a while to heal.
That feather-head horse was okay a-course,
    but that saddle sure was a different deal.

So ends my tale of the day I did sail
    offa mare with brains of manure.
Now, my horses I know, so that fact I'll forgo,
    but this lesson I learned was never truer.

Be sure of your mount, and NEVER discount,
    the words of the boss that are spoken.
But, if borrow you must, a company saddle to trust …
    THEN, BY GAWD,
        PICK ONE THAT'S NEVER BEEN BROKEN!

I don't know what ever happened to that saddle, but I'm sure that my friend, Carson Scheller, who owned the Bar S Bar Ranch in Los Alamos, California, probably had more than one laugh from seein' that ol' thing fly apart.

William S. Hart

Though he was born of genteel blood,
    he never knew or lived the part,
    for the west was also in the blood
    of the cowboy actor, William S. Hart.

On the banks of many Midwest rivers
    his boyhood was spent and he grew
    to love the Indian and his ways,
    so he learned the language of the Sioux.

Young William's father was a miller,
    o'er mountains and plains he did roam,
    in search of the perfect mill site
    where they could settle and make a home.

Then his mother lost her health
    as the hard life took its toll,
    so, she went east for a doctor's care,
    and to refurbish her worn soul.

William had shirked his schoolin',
    while roamin' 'round with his dad;
    he spent most of his idle time
    toppin' off horses that were bad.

Many times the family split
    to be reunited, as 'cross the country they trailed;
    his father never found the perfect mill site,
    and soon his health had failed.

Bill had to work to help his family,
    just so they could make ends meet;
    then he joined an athletic club,
    and found he had quick flyin' feet.

He also grew to love the theater,
    saw all the plays he held so dear.
    Then one day he began to see himself
    in pursuit of an acting career.

He had found he was torn between two loves,
    and a great decision he had to face:
    Was he to pursue an acting career,
    or was he meant to race?

Acting ambitions soon won out,
    but he was turned away at many an agent's door;
    the theater proved to be his true love,
    though it kept him broke and poor.

So, through the maze he struggled,
    and social stairs he seemed to shun;
    then a cowboy act came 'round his way,
    with chaps, spurs and gun.

Then one Sunday he was invited
    to a great party on the hill;
    he finally agreed that he would go,
    though somewhat against his will.

When he arrived, it was a costume ball,
    why he wasn't told, now no one knows.
    The host hid him out, then sent someone to go
    and fetch his cowboy clothes.

"Cowboy Bill" was quite a hit
    there among the Carmens, Cleopatras, and queens;
    he never had been much of a drinker,
    but hit the punch bowl that night it seems.

In the crowd there was some rascals,
    who were wishin' to have some fun,
    and figgered if they pestered Bill long enough,
    they'd get him to fire off his gun.

So, Bill cut loose with both barrels,
    the hand-painted ceiling caught some lead;
    all the queens and Carmens vanished,
    as the gun smoke curled 'round his head.

He started quite a stampede,
    with the gunfire's booming sound,
    the orchestra quickly disbanded,
    and the fiddles crashed to the ground.

Soon, he got a letter from the hostess,
    Bill figgered she was hoppin' mad,
    but she said he'd been the life of the party,
    and it was the best one she'd ever had!

Bill had raised havoc with the ceiling,
    but she didn't really seem to mind,
    although, the artist who did it was in Holland,
    and a little hard to find.

She said all of her guests had loved him,
    and he'd been just loads of fun;
    so, would he please come back again,
    and be sure to bring his gun.

Then, on a more intimate level,
   the hostess asked of him, "Dear Bill,
   of the seven ladies at the party you proposed to,
   please tell me if you will,

Were you serious about any of them,
   or were your offers made in jest?
   They're all my friends, I must stay neutral,
   but if you need my help I'll do my best!"

Bill studied hard till his acting improved,
   and his work caused quite a stir;
   he played the part of Romeo,
   and Messala in Ben Hur.

A few year later, while in Chicago,
   fate glanced mournfully his way,
   for an event took place that haunted Bill
   from then until his dyin' day.

He received a wire from sister Mary,
   that caused him to cry with ragged breath.
   his dear mother who lived upon the hill,
   had joined his father in the arms of death.

The season had just opened
   and no understudies were yet known,
   so, the play would surely fail,
   if he left it now alone.

He was deeply torn from within,
   and right or wrong he did not know;
   but, in the end, though he thought it was his duty,
   to her side he did not go.

His sister stood a woeful girl,
    with gloom on a blustery spring day,
    and saw their mother to the graveyard,
    to beside their father lay.

By the graves of their father and sister Lotta,
    and a little brother born in the West,
    she took the task to hand alone,
    and laid their mother there to rest.

A few years slowly passed
    and Bill acted out his parts ...
    like Sherlock Holmes and the Virginian;
    he reached out and touched many hearts.

Then, one day in Cleveland it happened,
    he saw a Western picture show.
    he thought that it was awful,
    and how it sold he didn't know.

The costumes were all wrong
    and the scenes were poor at best,
    but through the crowds Bill saw the light,
    'I'm an actor, and I know the West!'

His ambitions quickly grew
    and soon the die had been cast;
    ideas came on him in hordes,
    finally it could pay, his Broadway past.

So, soon he was off to California,
    and ne'r once did he look back;
    with him went his loving sister Mary,
    and his great friend the bulldog, Mack.

So, he made his motion pictures,
 those silent Westerns that brought him fame;
 "The Bargain," "On The Midnight Stage,"
 and "Tumbleweeds," just a few to name.

He got into many a fierce jangle,
 and he stepped on quite a few toes,
 to uphold all true representation
 of those silent Western heroes.

His friend, Charlie Russell, the artist
 he'd met up Montana way,
 had given him a picture he'd pain'ted of Bill,
 and it's still here with us today.

Bill talked long and hard with Charlie,
 to get him to go to New York one day;
 he thought he should meet some other artists,
 he did, and soon was on his way.

Bill took him and his wife Nancy
 to see a friend, Mr. Clark,
 the Sunday editor of the *New York Herald*,
 and then Charlie made his mark.

Charlie Russell was a Western man,
 and Bill could hardly get him to speak,
 but Mr. Clark gave Charlie a full page
 in the Sunday *Herald* that week.

Then Russell pain'ted a picture,
 a cowboy scene of Western ways.
 Nancy sold it for three hundred dollars,
 and could hardly talk for days!

Some time later,
    on the 25th of June in the year of '26,
    Bill Hart was invited to Montana,
    to the site of Custer's bad fix.

He spoke of that day with great reverence,
    for the old Indian country was his love.
    Before him were warriors and soldiers,
    as eagles soared in blue skies above.

The bronzed Seventh Cavalry on prancing mounts,
    fired volleys o'er graves of dead.
    The sound of "Taps" softly echoed,
    and the death song hung in heart and head.

Bill spoke to Native American brothers,
    as out on their feathered heads he gazed;
    he spoke to them in the tongue of the Sioux,
    and they were bewildered and amazed.

Later, he asked old Chief White Bull,
    who was there at Custer's last stand,
    to describe what happened that day
    as he fought for the right to his land.

The old chief could not even answer,
    said, "There was so much dust in the air,
    just fighting and screaming and misery,
    dying soldiers and braves everywhere."

Then Bill asked, "What were you thinking
   through the battle around you so wild?"
   The old chief answered with dignity,
   though his words were like those of a child,

"I was thinking of my sweetheart,
   how it seemed it wasn't right,
   that the dust was so thick all around,
   she couldn't see me bravely fight."

Back in Hollywood, Bill had many problems,
   'bout like any old country boy would.
   It seemed he, too, was like his father,
   honest, and too open for his own good.

To Bill, a handshake was his honor,
   but now it wasn't enough anymore,
   and those old foes, jealousy and greed,
   were lurking there behind the door.

And though he made many great pictures,
   directed and starred in them all,
   he went down before the Hollywood grind,
   but he went down ridin' tall.

Before the era of "talkies" began
   Bill decided he'd had his fill,
   and with his sister Mary
   and his horse Fritz, retired to his ranch on the hill.

He became a stalwart to the community,
   helped bring the education level higher.
   Once, he was seen in a bucket brigade,
   helping to put out a building fire.

He left La Loma de los Vientos,
   as he called his mansion on the hill,
   to the people of Santa Clarita,
   it was so declared there in his will.

His Western art and guns and blankets
   are there now for us all to see,
   just the way Bill had wanted,
   there is no charge, the tour is free.

Let's all take our hats off,
   to a great man we all hold dear,
   a legend who left his mark on America,
   that says … "William S. Hart was here."

∿ ∿

This was co-written with my old friend, Les Buffham. Giving credit where credit is due, he came up with the idea and the first draft. I recorded this poem and donated the tapes to the William S. Hart Museum to help raise funds for them. My actual contribution was relatively small, but we felt it should be included in this book to pay homage to a great American, to acknowledge the historic relevance of exactly who William S. Hart was, and to remember the important role he played in not only Santa Clarita, but also to the whole world.

Fiddler and the Gray

There was a time long ago, when our history did possess,
    a land of great horses, and tales of the West.
When men of daring courage, and thrill for the speed,
    would gamble their life on the fate of a steed.

Twas in White Clay, Nebraska, south of Pine Ridge Reservation,
    gathered the white men and half-breed, and the Sioux Indian nation.
After the Johnson County Wars they witnessed one day,
    when Jim Dahlman's "Fiddler" raced Joe Larvie's gray.

"Fiddler" was a blood bay, by way of Texas he's trailed,
    from the Pecos to Wyoming, and never had he failed.
Up the Chisholm Trail to Ogallala, he'd won every purse,
    spawning tales of a legend, in song and in verse.

All the outfits gathered, from the Driskills and Flying V,
    the Hashknife and Turkey Track, they'd all come to see.
This great burst of speed from Dahlman's proud bay,
    would silence yet another challenge, this one ... from Larvie's gray.

The Texans were rudely brash, promising some hot lead,
    for whoever rode the gray surely would be found dead.
Jack Russell was the gray's handler, rider and trainer,
    but he'd bowed out from fear, for a family man's somewhat saner.

Despair quickly set in through the camp of the Larvie horse,
    with no one brave enough to ride the six-hundred-yard course.
Intimidation had proved quite effective, from the cowboys so shady,
    when up the forefront stepped a wrangler … little Tom Brady.

Tom said, "I'll ride the gray, and I'll win you can bet.
    I'll not be bothered by some loud idle threat.
But, I'll ride not for riches, of this I'll confess,
    but for the hand of Joe Larvie's daughter, and her love to possess.

The crowd gathered early, the betting ground covered two acres,
    wagering horses and land, and money from all takers.
"Big Bat Pourier" laid down a thousand on Larvie's spirited gray,
    'twas a mountain of wealth and riches that the winner would pay.

It would be a fine haul for an outlaw like "Fly Speck Bill,"
    or Dunc Blackburn might steal it, just for the thrill.
But, a thousand guns guarded all the bettors' winning pool;
    to rob this mint of treasure, would surely take a fool.

The day of the race, the crowd came from far and wide,
    from ranches and villages, o'er the hills they did ride.
Soldiers and Indians, and sporting ranchers with cattle,
    with all their ladyfolk dain'tily mounted sidesaddle.

Joe Larvie's wagon was placed at the race finish line,
  with his youngest of French-blooded daughters so fine.
Her piercing eyes shone bright, and young Brady was heard to say,
  "For her ... I'll risk a bullet ... so, I'll surely ride the gray."

Horses crowded along the track, with more than one kicking,
  amidst a flurry of return strikes, and flared nostril nippings.
All quieted their mounts with sharp cuts from the reins,
  and smothered remarks from cursing lips so profane.

Jim Dahlman rode "Fiddler" with quiet pride to the track,
  Rebel yells filled the air as the Indians meekly stepped back.
A look of concern 'oer their red faces did appear,
  as one lone Indian emerged from the crowd in the rear.

It was "Young Horse," the mustanger, known to all around;
  he walked onto the track and placed his blanket on the ground.
He knelt down on one knee, and his hands he did thrust,
  with the palms facing downward, into the powdered dust.

He muttered what seemed to be an ancient Indian saying,
    as he traced little circles in the dirt, and started praying.
He rose and said to all the spectators standing near,
    "LET THEM RACE! …
        BUT LET THE RED HORSE RUN PAST HERE!"

Tom Brady rode the excitable gray, rearing high against the bit,
    prancing like a springy deer, with flying foam of spit.
He eyed Larvie's young daughter, touched his hat with his quirt,
    while Dahlman and the veteran "Fiddler" just quietly sat.

The gray jumped twice, like any hot blood in its prime,
    then they both stood silent for an instant … frozen in time.
The gun CRACKED! Fiddler shot one full length ahead
    the gray took to the chase, and down the track they sped!

Brady whipped furiously, through the heel dust to the flying tail,
    then to the flank, as the pebbles pounded like giant hail!
Evened up to Dahlman's stirrup, the gray made his bid for first,
    but "Fiddler" laid his ears back, and turned on that famous burst!

Brady rode Indian fashion, whipped him from side to side,
    as the blood bay opened up to lengthen out his stride!
Young Tom screamed in the gray's ear, a Sioux Indian war cry,
    then he shot ahead, and the two horses began to fly!

Neck and neck they ran, in whiteish dust thick as fog,
    both quirts a blur, as they continued to flog!
They ran like the blizzard of Dakota, on winds they did ride,
    so close together they could be covered by one buffalo hide!

But, for all the whip and spur that was put to the gray,
    the heroic bay, "Fiddler," began pulling away!
At first, the width of a finger, then a full length, and more,
    through the dust and the wind, and the crowd's mighty roar!

They reached the spot where the Indian had touched the track,
    then "Fiddler" broke stride, and faltered in his attack!
He shifted his gait, and ran wide with a jump,
    as Dahlman spurred his hide, and put the quirt to his rump!

The gray took the lead, with his belly low to the ground,
    like a coyote running scared, from a rabid bloodhound!
Then, "Fiddler" exploded 'neath leather, with the force of a gale,
    NEVER had a horse run so fast … but all to no avail …

For the gray crossed the line, to stave off the bay's rally,
    running so hard, Brady couldn't stop him till they were down
    in the valley.
Dahlman's face was ghostly white, and he was the first to admit,
    he didn't know what happened, but that was the first time
    "Fiddler" … quit.

The Texans were half-mad, and in quiet state of shock.
    How could a heathens magic affect such fine racing stock?
The Indians clucked their ponies home, 'cross the river late that night,
    loaded down with all their booty, from the horsemen that were white.

But, what's stranger you see, is Tom Brady's unlucky fate,
    for he failed to win the heart, of the Larvie beauty there in wait.
Seemed she preferred the Agency Blacksmith, who never had won,
    such riches for her mother's people, on just a race he'd won.

There was a time long ago, when our history possessed,
    a land of great horses, and tales of the West.
When a young man of daring courage, and thrill for the speed,
    lost the love of his heart ... on the fate of a steed.

              ❧   ☙

One of the most poignant documentaries of the West ever recorded was by Mari Sandoz in her book, *The Cattlemen*. Not only is this book great reading, but it is full of historically correct events and factual, eyewitness accounts of many occurrences that helped forge this country's early years. This story was so powerful, I felt compelled to put it into poetry form. The credit goes to Mari Sandoz, though, for her vivid descriptions brought it to life. A copy of this poem was presented to, and now hangs in, the Mari Sandoz Museum in Nebraska.

The Last Coyote

He sits, perched on a hill, backlit by the moon,
the last of the coyotes, howlin' his mournful tune.

Time was, when he ran wild, not too may years ago,
in countless numbers he roamed, seeking out his foe.

The ranchers called him the devil, for the calves were his prey;
they'd just as soon see him rot in hell, if they could have their way.

To a farmer, he wasn't much better, he'd eat anything to survive
a prize hen, a good workin' dog, dang near anything alive.

His song kept a cowboy company, on the lonely plain at night;
it was somehow, kinda romantic ... as long as he wasn't on the fight.

He was the scourge of the earth, most all would agree,
runnin' in packs filled with death, destroying everything he would see.

We shot him and trapped him, and put a price on his hide;
we hung him on the wall, and admired our bounty with pride.

Then, progress took over, and with the dawning of a modern day,
we drove him further into the hills, with all our suburban ways.

We cut down his trees, then crushed his home, and left him nothin'
    to eat;
so, he came down to greet us, where house and fences meet.

We found him in shopping centers, he even killed a child,
his rabid heart filled with murder, this creature runnin' wild.

So, we bulldozed him in, surrounded him with concrete and steel,
we left him nothin' … now, he stalks his last meal.

His numbers they have dwindled, and with each passing day,
we find a more effective method, to clear him from our way.

What a price he's paid, so we can be civilized,
he's damn near extinction, or haven't we realized;

that perched upon a hill, singing one final tune,
sits the very last coyote, howlin' at the moon.

    Some people have misconstrued the meaning behind this
piece as being some sort of environmental statement, or
that I'm a "tree-huggin' bunny lover" or somethin'. Fact is,
it's just an observation. Many things in the West are
changin', that's reality; and I'm no more in favor of
crusading for the coyote than I am protesting against
bovine gas expelling into the air.

The Horse Psychologist

A lotta folks raised 'round horses
    figger there's nothin' that's plainer,
than to subsidize your income a little …
    why not be a horse trainer?

I know that's true in my case,
    but my story don't be misconstruin';
I ain't no Pat Parelli or Ray Hunt,
    but I danged shore know what I'm doin'.

There really ain't no right or wrong way,
    just whatever works for you and the horse,
as long as you ain't foolish or cruel,
    and always keep an open mind a-course.

Anyway, I get this call from a friend,
    whose horse I trained beyond a doubt.
Says she's havin' a little problem with her Arab mare,
    and would I please stop by and check it out.

I said, "Yep," and I followed her directions,
    and turned left at the tennis court,
then I pulled into the …
    Happy Horse Haven Hotel Sports Center Equestrian Resort!

Well, she comes out to greet me a-wearin' stretch pants,
    knee boots, and this black helmet sorta like a bubble.
I said, "Howdy, ma-am, I'm the trainer.
    What seems to be the trouble?"

She said, "I've spent plenty of time and money,
    havin' this horse diagnosed and evaluated.
I've sent her to a 'horse psychologist',
    so, now she can be properly educated."

Well, I politely swallered my laugh,
    and watched her handle the horse for awhile.
I already had a purty good idea what the problem was,
    but her temper I didn't wanna rile.

She says, "She bites when you feed her an apple,
    she'll take your finger off with the core!"
I told her, "Well, don't feed her by hand, Miss,
    that's what feed barrels are for."

She said, "She's impossible to lead,
    and her ground manners are quite rude!"
I told her, "Well, snap her head and MAKE her listen,
    and stop treatin' her like you're a dude."

She says, "The PSYCHOLOGIST SAYS ...
    she won't go in the wash rack
    because she suffers from hypertension!"
I said, "Ma-am, keep her head straight and be patient,
    and use the end a-that lead rope to get her attention."

She says, "The PSYCHOLOGIST SAYS ...
    she's got separation anxiety,
    and the trailer door you'll never close!"
I said, "Well, I believe I can fix that in 'bout 10 minutes, ma-am,
    with a stud chain 'cross her honry ol' nose."

She says, "The PSYCHOLOGIST SAYS …
    she's got an identity crisis,
    that's why she won't stand still when you mount!"
I said, "Well, I've found that a strategically, well-placed size 10-boot
    is somethin' a little hard for 'em to discount."

Now, those of you who've been 'round horses,
    by now might be bustin' a gut;
but, it's a little hard to educate someone 'bout horses in an hour,
    so, I'm stuck there, just tryin' to reason with this New Age nut.

But, that's when things got a little ugly,
    as she looked down and saw the spurs on my boots.
She says, "You're not going to use THOSE things on her!
    How could you be such a BRUTE?"

I said, "Well, they're not for killin' horses, ma-am,
    but, they come in right handy if they start to buck,
or if they need a little proddin',
    well, I've found that they brings me lottsa luck."

She says, "I think your methods are quite barbaric!
    How could you be so ruthless, and so mean?"
I said, "Well, cowboys like me've been abusin' horses for centuries;
    matter of fact, ma-am, it's quite routine."

I said, "In all due respect, ma-am,
    I'm gonna give you some advice … and all for free.
You obviously don't know what the Hell you're doin',
    or elst you wouldn't even be tryin' to talk to someone like me."

"You find someone else to train that bubble-headed horse,
      and as far as your friend, the HORSE PSYCHOLOGIST,
well, with all the hot air and manure he's tryin' to feed you,
      you might wanna find yourself a proctologist!"

≈   ≋

I was the third trainer this gal had interviewed, and she
found two more after me. Apparently, all of us had the
same opinion and evaluation of her situation. The following
spring, I was at a team penning and ran into her, and she
had a cute little pair of equestrian spurs on. I asked her how
her mare was doin', and she said everything was goin' great
since she had "got ahold" of her horse. Some people are just
slow learners, huh?

Time to Ride

Some call it sport, with one fleeting moment of glory.
Others say it's just a game, but, that's only half the story.

More than a few think it's crazy, to gamble on one eight-second ride,
tempting mortal life, and loss of limb, where fear and guts collide.

To them that don't do it, well, it might be just a show,
but, to a cowboy that lives it, it's everything … it's rodeo.

It's a living legacy, and history, a tribute to our past;
it's Americana, and our heritage, like a die that has been cast.

It's 1200 pounds of buckin' fury, and a buzzin' in our head,
the glass-eyed euphoria of the beast, and the ghost of every cowboy dead.

It's the smell of leather, and stench of sweat, and a quiver deep inside,
it's riggin' wrapped tight, and loss of breath, when the cowboy nods
    … outside.

It's your own private war, with only one winner to the fight,
and every part of your body goes numb, when the two of you hit
    daylight.

It's a twist and a turn, and the glimmering shank of steel,
an eternity of soul-searching, that only a cowboy can feel.

You go on luck and instinct, and pray to God you're the best;
then the clock and fate take over, the bronc does the rest.

If you stay on his back long enough, you can call a truce,
with the pickup man beside you, you finally turn him loose.

But, there will be another day, when you'll have to prove you can win,
'cause you're cowboy, through and through … it's time to ride again.

It's Good to Be Alive

I wonder how many times I've rode this trail,
 and stopped to meditate,
 what a lucky man I am to breathe this air,
 a fact I won't debate.

The good Lord's blessed me with all of my senses,
 and I've never questioned why;
 I figger, he always knows what he's doin',
 so my blessings I don't deny.

The eyes that he gave me are his windows,
 to witness all the world,
 like the flight of an eagle, the birth of a colt,
 or the hair of a pretty girl.

I've seen cattle bedded down at night,
 and thunderclouds roll my way.
 I've watched the rainbow follow the downpour,
 and the dawning of a sunlit day.

My ears have heard the trickling of a cool mountain stream,
 and a baby's sweet lullaby;
 the wind whipping through the prairie grass,
 and song of the lone wolf's cry.

I've listened long and hard to the stillness of the night,
 and many a cowboy sing;
 the sound of horseshoe, hammer and anvil,
 and the chow bell when it rings.

I've tasted the best water put on earth,
    and ol' camp cookie's stew;
      that first hot cup of coffee in the mornin',
    and some good tobacco to chew.

I've swallered acres of dust and kegs of whiskey,
    till I thought I'd die,
      but nothin' will ever beat the flavor
    of a big ol' piece of hot apple pie.

I've smelled cowhide burnin' from the hot iron,
    and honeysuckle in the trees;
      the subtle scent of juniper and pine
    just a-blowin' through the breeze.

Now, the odor of a corral, some might detest,
    but, to me it's mighty good.
      I don't reckon I'd trade places with any man alive,
    even if I could.

But some of my senses I can't really define,
    'cause they're somewhere deep inside,
      like the sight of Old Glory on the Fourth of July,
    or an early mornin' ride.

Just knowin' that I'm free,
    and I have a purpose, makin' a livin' off this land;
      it's sorta a sense of peace bunkin' with Mother Nature,
    so I've come to understand,

That I reckon I'm luckier than most,
    and how I've learned to survive,
      but, I figger I'm like any cowboy with all his senses ...
    it shore is good to be alive!

Lane Frost

There's been many a tale told around a campfire,
 of cowboys bein' tossed,
but none can compare to the true life story
 of the great bullrider ... Lane Frost.

Now, some might say ol' Freckles Brown,
 on "Tornado" was the best,
but history always repeats itself,
 so, another cowboy was put to the test.

He came out of Oklahoma from stout and hearty stock
 his daddy cowboyed with Casey Tibbs.
His pride and courage was family breeding,
 and no one loved him like his mama Elsie did.

He weren't exactly the classic figure for bullridin'
 but, that kinda cowboyin's done from the heart.
It takes sheer guts, and divine obsession'
 that's what set Lane Frost apart.

He started out as a pup, right outta school,
 and got his card in '83.
Everyone knew he had what it takes, this rookie runner-up,
 to be one of the best we'd ever see.

But, like any bullrider, Lane had his hard times,
 like Del Rio in '84.
They gave him the "Hard Luck Award" and no buckle,
 just ground money and no score.

Or, how about the times he lost on "Mr. T,"
   three draws he never rode.
Seemed that ball of thunder had Lane's number ...
   each time he would explode.

But, the great ones find a way to win,
   and just like ol' Freckles Brown,
Lane found his groove and got on a roll,
   and finally earned his crown.

In '87, he became world champion,
   and showed us all just how good he could ride.
That feller had a way of gettin' off-a bull sometimes,
   that would leave you breathless all inside.

Then came "Red Rock" in '88,
   from John Growney's Red Bluff string,
a buck-off, with best against best,
   to see who was the king.

311 times that bull had throwed the cowboys,
   and not one had ever stayed atop;
but, Lane rode "Red Rock," the great athlete, 4 out of 7,
   and became the cream of the crop.

In the finals of '89 in Cheyenne,
   he scored an 85,
ridin' a bull called ... "Tendin' To Business,"
   the one he wouldn't survive.

He horned him in the side,
   and his rib cut into the vein,
but, any cowboy who rides the circuit knows ...
   that's just part of the game.

Like all champions that walk among us,
    it's not just the accolades they've won,
that sets them apart from the rest of us,
    with all the deeds they've done.

It's their heart and their inspiration
    that makes us all strive;
and Lane, well, he had that special somethin',
    so his memory will forever be alive.

He always had time for a friend,
    and what a smile he had;
so, for God gracing us with him for 25 years,
    I reckon we all should be mighty glad.

It's not just Kellie, or his folks,
    that he left far behind;
it's every rodeo fan that loved him,
    and every cowboy ready to unwind.

A little piece of us all
    died on that arena ground,
and another one like Lane Frost,
    will never, ever be found.

The rodeo lights are dim,
    for a legend has been lost;
but, he was cowboy, all the way to the bone,
    and one helluva bullrider .... Lane Frost.

Shortly after Lane's death, I spoke with his folks, Clyde and Elsie. After reading this poem, they graciously agreed to let me release it on tape as a tribute, on the condition that I would put in the piece that Lane believed that "Red Rock" was the greatest athlete he had ever rode.

Ranchers Against Twine

Any cowboy, rancher, buckaroo,
    or just a hand for hire,
will be the first to tell you what built the West …
    by Gawd, it was BAILIN' WIRE!

Now, back in the old days,
    it was just plumb common sense,
to use whatever you had on hand,
    to mend that broken fence.

You could secure down the stack
    on the ol' pot-belly stove,
or use it to tighten anything,
    where a nail couldn't be drove.

It was used to tie the windows open,
    at the first sign of spring,
and to hold the door shut in winter,
    from all the snow it would bring.

You could fix a chair, route a pipe,
    repair a hinge, or clean a gun.
Shoot, there wasn't anything
    a piece a-bailin' wire couldn'a done.

It's held many clutch and muffler
    on an old pickup truck,
and helped danged near every rancher
    cut a corner and save a buck.

But, it seems some fool
    is always tryin' to fix somethin' that ain't broke,
so, they came up with somethin' to replace bailin' wire,
    man, what a joke!

Nowadays, when you get your alfalfa,
    it's wrapped up in this bright orange string!
You know, I don't think it's environmentally safe,
    and with it, you can't fix a durn thing!

So, I've decided to join the R.A.T. organization ...
    "Ranchers Against Twine,"
and I'll start seedin' my own hay,
    so I won't have to look at that neon line.

Hopefully, in the future,
    I won't have to deal with that string I hate,
'cause the cows just end up eatin' it,
    while I'm tryin to fix a broken gate!

    Did you ever wonder what folks do with all that twine?
I've seen it wrapped on corral fence posts, stacked up like
wax on a bee hive, and I've even heard people make tack
and halters out of it. I don't think I'd wanna put that stuff
on my horse and have all the boys say, "Nice bridle!"

Goodbye Ol' Friend

As I rode down the twenty mile road out of town to Tom Jenkins' place, the Colorado winter was just beginnin' to set in. Half sleet, half snow, and all cold. The mist risin' off the tree line, like a painter's canvas, conjured up forty years worth of memories.

Tom Jenkins was a top hand, and even though I figgered him to be over 70, he'd still do to ride the river with. That man knew more cowography than any man I'd ever run across, and he had more gravel in his gizzard than any ten men alive. I reckon most-a what I ever learned was from Tom, and what I learned on my own was 'cause I didn't listen to him from the get-go. Of course, everything he taught me wasn't of the bovine nature, you understand; for you see, even though his book learnin' was limited, he was quite a philosopher. He could judge a man's worth, was as honest as the day was long and, above all, loved everything 'bout bein' a cowboy, includin' the loneliness.

Tom first took me on when I was a button of seven or eight, I don't rightly remember. All I ever knew was my Daddy was a grub line rider and Mama was a calico queen who run off with some card mechanic somewhere down in Texas. Growin' up my first ten years or so, we was a-bouncin' from one cow camp to another. The country was still wide open then and most cowmen had plenty of space, so there was always plenty of work for a good contract buster like Tom Jenkins.

My education began with doin' chores for the coosie. Keepin' the chip box filled with prairie coal, makin' sure there was always hot Arbuckle for the crew, haulin' the sourdough keg, and totin' the war bags to the wagon and such. When I wasn't runnin' errands for that ol' hash slinger, I watched Tom do his stuff, and little by little, I learned 'bout cow savvy, horsemanship and range manners. Eventually, Tom got the trail boss to give me the job of wranglin' the remuda horses.

When I's 'bout ten, Tom gave me my first mount. Years later, I figgered it was meant to be a joke but, as I said, Tom Jenkins never did nothin' without a reason, and that ol' horse was another lesson in life for me. She was a broomtail claybank dun, with a fiddle head, lady-broke, that forged when she trotted. A puddin' footed, pecker-necked dink you wouldn't use for crow bait, but I loved that ol' nag. Tom had given me two lessons in one with that ol' hay burner. First of all, "You can judge a man by the horse he rides," and second, "Man is the only animal that can be skinned more than once."

Tom never was much of a talker, he was a doer. But, as we traveled the Santa Fe Trail, then north up to Wyoming and Montana, many a caballero with slack in the jaw met his match with ol' Tom. I remember one time in Nevada, we had hired on with this shirt-tail outfit waitin' for the spring thaw so's we could push north. There were only three other punchers, and one was a chesty borracho named Claymore who had a terminal case of bottle fever and was shore in the lead when tongues was give out. Now, this feller weren't exactly loaded with a bucket fulla smarts anyhow, but by the time he loaded up on bug juice, he'd get so stupid he couldn't drive a nail in a snowbank.

We was layin' out lick blocks on the mesa when this fool runs out of his gut-warmer, and his tongue swelled up like a tater in his mouth, he was so dry. So, Tom, who was workin' on a real good mad anyhow, stopped to cool his saddle, and decides to fill up his John B. with snow, then mixes in some salt shavin's for the loudmouth cowboy. Now, even though Claymore was so dumb he couldn't teach a hen to cluck, I didn't think he was such an idiot that he would drink from another man's hat, but he did! Needless to say, the ride back to camp was a quiet one. As we unsaddled the ponies, Tom says to Claymore, "The bigger the mouth ... the better it looks when it's shut!"

By the time I was in my early teens, I had traveled most of the country west of the "Big Muddy" with Tom Jenkins. Polishin' your britches on saddle leather don't necessarily make you a cowboy, and everywhere we'd light I learned more 'bout cowboyin', and even more 'bout life. Ridin' them trails with Tom filled my hours and head with all a man would ever need to know. "Success is the size of the hole a man leaves after he dies," he told me; and even though we always seemed to have hard chink in our jeans, we weren't exactly flush all the time either, but we always got by. Poverty depends an awful lot on a man's state of mind ... not just what he's got.

My first real saddle job came in the "big thicket" country of east Texas when I's 'bout fifteen. By then, Tom had taught me to throw a line with the best of 'em, and a-course I finally had me a good peggin' pony, a fan-tail grulla that he'd broke for me. That man could iron the humps out in three saddles on any outlaw alive. We hung on with that outfit for two years, me workin' as a brush popper and Tom snappin' broncs. I never really took to kickin' leppys outta that thicket, but it shore taught me how to throw a small overhand toss, and it damn shore toughened up my hide.

When spring came, we'd do our share of doctorin', then burn 'em, snub 'em, and boot 'em and start all over again. The ticks were as big as silver dollars, and we'd lose 'bout 100 head each year to Spanish Fever. By the time we pushed on to Arizona though, I was a cow puncher who really had the bark on.

Headin' west that year was one of the best of my life. On top of havin' great weather, and a caboodle of work, the Cowboy Turtle Association had just begun and organized rodeos were springin' up everywhere. We musta hit 'bout ten rodeos that summer, and ol' Tom was always in the money. Oh, I did purtty fair I reckon, but I shore drew my share of jugheads, too! Because Tom was a bronc buster by trade, he got more'n getaway money each time he rode. To this day, I reckon people are still talkin' 'bout that time in Yuma when he rode a skewbald wall-eyed mankiller called "Widow Maker." Now, that horse was known to be a runaway bucker, and a weedy spinner, so you never knew what he was gonna do. He'd already killed one cowboy by a-throwin' back in the chute ... a bonafide outlaw that was real snakey and mean. Tom was a purty easy goin' sorta fella, and he knew the only way to ride that bastard was to pump hisself fulla vinegar, so, after he set his riggin', he reached over and bit a piece a-ear right off that hunk a-livin' lightnin'. All hell broke loose, and when they hit the daylight that horse blows the plug and commenced to burnin' the breeze. Then he jumped up and goes to cloud-huntin' and come undone every which way, justa foggin' for all he's worth. Ol' Tom just kept combin' his hide, and diggin' in his guthooks like there was no tomorrow. "STAY WITH HIM," we all yelled, and a-course Tom had no intention of kissin' the ground and chewin' gravel. Well, friends I mean to tell ya, this weren't no ten second ride. He stayed with that hell-raiser for nigh on two minutes and never grabbed the apple once, a-whoopin' and a-hollerin' the whole ride! Finally, he bails out, spits out that piece a-ear, tips his hat to the crowd, and everyone just came unglued.

Ol' Tom just sauntered away like it was nothin' … but I knew he was as happy as a hog in a melon patch. Yeah, he shore 'nuff was a rodeo man, and' 'bout the cleanest sitter I ever saw.

I reckon the best memories I have of Tom was the next four or five years we spent up north. Ranchers were beginnin' to fence in by then, and me and Tom were on the last of the great cross-country cattle drives there was. No chute brandin', or doctorin' from a pickup, just good hard cowboy work with the top hands left from the old days, in plenty of open range.

I was full-growed by then, and could hang and rattle with the best of 'em, but Tom Jenkins was gettin' a little long in the tooth, and didn't exactly travel like a colt no more. The last two years in Wyoming, Tom got the job as Big Sugar for the outfit, and I was his right hand. Sometimes, he'd ride night herd with me, just for the company. Now, contrary to dime store novels, anyone knows that most cowboys don't sing like a bird ... and Tom fit into that category just fine! Why, when he went to singin' to 'em to keep 'em bedded down, he had a voice like a burro with a bad cold, and could drive all the coyotes outta the country! His songs were a might shy on melody and a heap strong on noise, but I reckon a man don't have to be no born vocalist to sing by hisself in the dark to a cow ... as long as he's got a clear conscience, and ain't a-hidin' out.

By the time I was twenty-one, me and ol' Tom were more than companeros. Sometimes we was so close, folks probably figgered we used the same toothpick, but I came to realize we were just cut from the same leather. One summer, we was pushin' steers, gettin' ready to cross the Snake River. We were drivin' a loose herd, tryin' to get 'em millin', and Tom and I were outriders. Some of the deacons had strayed off into an arroyo, so we heads off to kick 'em out. Now, ordinarily Tom stuck to a saddle like a postage stamp, so when I sees his sorrel spook and start to pitchin', I didn't think much of it. Bu, then he blew a stirrup and that cayuse comes to one helluva whoa, and flung him off. Tom's ol' legs were a-kickin' 'round in the air like a migratin' bullfrog in flight. Tom pops up, airin' his lungs at that featherhead, when all of a sudden, a timber wolf on the peck comes a-screamin' outta the trees and unloads on his pony. That hell-bent lobo tore into that horse and laid his guts out quick, and was goin' for Tom when I took him down with my Winchester.

We could hear a whole pack a-them devils too dang
close, and Tom didn't even wanna fetch his saddle offa that
carcass, so he does a flyin' mount behind me and
commenced to huggin' leather as we lit outta there pronto
… with alla-them steers in hot pursuit! This proved to be
one a-them days when nothin' went right, my friend, 'cause
as we were headin' south breakin' brush, we ran smack
through a den of jumpy polecats … and they sprayed us up
one side and down the other! Now, only a fool argues with
a cook, a mule, or a skunk, so we just kept makin' tracks
with ol' Tom doubled up on back of me. By the time we
reached camp, all we wanted was a good wash, some chuck
and a dream sack. We shore took more'n our fair share of
good natured proddin' from the boys, but skunk juice don't
wash out that easy, so for the next few days them cowhands
went 'round us like we were a swamp! We shore did stink,
and the ramrod made us swap with two of the tally men for
a spell so's we would be downwind from the outfit.

The followin' winter we hooked up with this floatin'
outfit in Montana, and after the late brandin' there weren't
much to do 'cept ride fence and chop ice, so me and Tom,
John Henry and Pete, spent a lotta time in town ragged out
in our Sunday best, tryin' our dangdest to support the local
cantinas. Drinkin' and swappin' lies is 'bout the only cure
for cabin fever in that country … that is, till the fightin'
starts 'round mid-March. It's a good time to work on your
tack, braid bosals and make hair bridles. When a "blue
norther" blows in Montana, and you're snowed in for weeks
at a time, you best be with good compadres, or you're in for
a heapa-trouble. You can practice buildin' loops, or play
cards if the company's right, and I reckon ol' Tom did more
talkin' that winter than he did in his whole life. When the
spring thaw came, Tom had convinced us all of one thing
though. "If God had intended for man to walk, He'd a-gave
him four feet, but He gave him two … one to put on each
side of a horse."

After that winter, cowboy work was startin' to get scarce,
and for the first time in my life, Tom Jenkins and I rode
separate trails. You go where the work is, and I took on as a
mill rider in Idaho, while Tom shoved south. He was still
one of the best damn "tie hard and fast" men around, and
landed on the Bell Ranch in New Mexico where he could
show the youngsters how to pull the trip and roll a calf.
Banks and co-ops were takin' over the cattle business, and
all the old-timers were startin' to see the writin' on the wall.
Tom and I crossed paths once every year or so for 'bout the
next fifteen years. Every time I'd see him, there'd be one more
line in that weathered ol' face. A little piece a-him died every
time a fence went up, or another section was taken from the
old ranches. He took it all in stride, though, even though
he knew his days as a point rider had long since vanished.

There wasn't an hour that went by that I didn't think 'bout that ol' buzzard and all that he meant to me. After all, we were so much alike that I'd come to understand on my own that ... horses might not do what machines can but dammit ... they shore can keep you company.

When I rode into Tom's place, I could see the old cabin had changed since I was there last spring. Even though he'd been slowed up by his boogered up ol' leg, he always kept things in purty good repair. The gate was open. That ol' dun horse was nowhere to be seen. Tom always greeted everyone out front wavin' the bean pot. Somethin' was wrong. "Tom," I yelled, as I stuck my head through the hole in the screen door. "Tom, you here?" Only the sound of slow heavy breathin' pierced the air from the back room a-that shack that was filled with forty years gatherin's. The mecate in his hands lay draped 'cross his sunken chest. "I cut Ol' Dunny loose this mornin'," he said, "but if I'da known you was a-comin' ... I'da just a-soon you took him on in your string." I knew he was gettin' ready to shake hands with Sain't Peter, and I was glad I was there ... but somehow ... I felt like I was intrudin'. "Remember that fiddle-head ol' dun I gave you?" he chuckled and coughed. He didn't have much try left in him, so I squeezed his hand and nodded. "You learned good ... cowboy," he said, as the life wheezed out a-him, a smile plastered on his salty ol' face. I sat there ... as motionless as him ... for more'n an hour ... wonderin' why I never told him how I really felt ... or why I never thanked him for givin' me my grit. But, I reckon before he crossed the great divide, he saw the look on my face ... and felt my hand. He knew ... he always knew. *Hasta la vista, amigo* ... goodbye ol' friend.

This story was inspired by Con Becker and a dozen other old timers. It's the recollections of those old cowboys, their stories and lives, rolled into one saga. Their way of life has disappeared in the last few years with their passing, but we should never forget those who came before us.

Land of Enchantment

A full moon hangs in the pitch black sky,
    as I ride for the top of the mountain so high.
This land of enchantment is unforgiving, yet kind,
    and a great sense of peace encircles my mind.

It's well below freezin', as I start toward the peak,
    and funnels of breath come out as I speak.
But, I'm dressed for the cold, and all warm inside,
    for a New Mexico winter mornin' trail ride.

The darkness of night turns a silky charcoal gray,
    and tufts of snow on the evergreens lay.
My horse plods along through the drifts that are deep,
    and icicles dangle from red rocks so steep.

The sky turns to mauve, then a soft misty pink;
    as a hawk screams above me, I pause just to think.
The mountains awake, breaking a silence serene,
    and I take in the vision that few men have seen.

The pink fades to indigo, then bright powder blue,
    and I sit on the mountain to take in the view.
My horse snickers loudly, at a creature in flight,
    and we both stare in awe at this heavenly sight.

The yellow sun bursts, on the valley below me,
    as a mother cow stirs, and bellows so lowly.
Adobes are speckled 'cross the pastel land,
    beholding a scene spectacular and grand.

Smoke curls from the chimney of a rancher's mornin' fire,
    and shadows are cast as the sun climbs higher.
Overwhelmed by this picture from so high above,
    I ponder my existence in this land that I love.

The land of enchantment, New Mexico Oh, how I adore thee,
    a patchwork blanket of nature that lies here before me.
I feel God gave me this to nurture my soul,
    where reality is timeless … like stories untold.

I love to watch the sunrise from this mountain top so high,
    and share the crisp, cold mornin' where majestic eagles fly.
The only thing better to do in this spot I have found,
    is ride up here in the evenin' … and watch the sun go down.

∾ ∾

I wrote this one winter mornin', high in the mountains
on the Taos Indian Reservation with my good friend,
Ceasario, who runs the Taos Indian Horse Ranch. I've had
some very special spiritual moments in that country, and
will forever be indebted to Ceasario for sharin' his land and
culture with me.

The Canyon Wind

Through the valleys of Santa Clarita,
    by the river that twists and bends,
lies the eternal lifeblood of California,
    in the blowing canyon winds.

They howled before the Chumash Indian
    had ever planted their first corn,
and they've whistled through the tree tops,
    before the West was ever born.

I've rode these valleys and canyons,
    for more than a few years,
and the winds have spoken to me,
    as they've twirled 'round my ears.

They speak of pioneers and settlers,
    and the ghosts of cowboys past;
they all live within the canyon wind,
    and forever more will last.

Somewhere between where old Newhall
    and Placerita Canyon has its start,
I've felt the eerie presence
    of the spirit of William S. Hart.

High above San Francisquito Canyon,
    I've rested my horse upon the peak,
as the wind carried voices of miners,
    talking of the gold they did seek.

Sometimes, it's just a breeze,
    that gently kisses across your face,
just Mother Nature's subtle reminder,
    of another time and forgotten place.

I look down on the UB Ranch,
    and the stables of the Amber Rose,
while riding trails above Farmer John's,
    tracking a rogue buck and his does.

The wind whispers of tragedy,
    back when Mullholland's Dam busted;
the dead seem to have reincarnated,
    in the wind their soul's intrusted.

Occasionally, I pause on the ridge,
    as the wind swallows up my mind,
and I feel the holy presence,
    of the secrets I've yet to find.

The wind takes me to Leona,
    through the sandy river bed,
winding through endless cattle trails,
    as the spirits dance in my head.

I drop down into Charlie Canyon,
    that's rich with dove and quail,
as the wind dies down a little,
    to a sweet hypnotic wail.

Joaquin Murietta and other banditos,
    with all the booty that they've carried,
seem to haunt the shadows of oak trees,
    where their treasure might be buried.

The Vasquez rocks of Aqua Dulce
   spiral upwards toward the skies,
there, the wind seems to chant in harmony,
   before it disappears and dies.

I've rode above Val Verde,
   in Hasley Canyon just at dusk,
where the wind brings scents of pinon,
   and the sagebrush smells of musk.

All across the Gilmour Ranch,
   from Castaic to Piru,
the beauty of the canyon winds
   is matched only by the view.

The winds are strange in summer,
   crisp and slightly cool,
yet, in winter they seem they're warmer,
   and your senses they can fool.

They have a pulse … they breathe …
   and their moods bring them to life;
sometimes, they're cruel and relentless …
   cutting … like a sharp knife.

The wind will show no mercy,
   as it chills you to the bone,
but, then it caresses your sense of longing,
   with a soothing low pitched moan.

It blows to infinity,
   it never starts and it never ends;
those of us who've befriended them,
   understand the canyon winds.

One gust that blew upon you,
    on a blustery winter day,
just might return and revisit you,
    when the blooms return in May.

They've gained their strength and power,
    from the souls of all the men,
who've lived down in the valleys,
    with the mighty canyon wind.

Like an overpowering sorceress,
    weaving a magic spell,
the winds control mere mortals,
    in the canyons where they dwell.

You become a part of them,
    and they a part of you,
as you share the common life force,
    from every wind that ever blew.

I know that life's eternal,
    like that of old cowboys past,
for in the mighty canyon winds,
    my soul will ever last.

Through the valleys of Santa Clarita,
    on trails that never end,
you'll find me in a hundred years
    … within the canyon wind.

I spent many years a-horseback in these canyons, ridges and valleys, puttin' a lot of wet blankets on young horses, and communing with nature. Shortly after writing this poem, the Santa Clarita valley selected me as their official Cowboy Poet Laureate. If it weren't for the durn earthquakes, I might still be there today.

Painted Lady

I rode into Cheyenne,
    some twenty years ago,
    dog-tired to the bone from the trail I'd been ridin',
    so I stopped at the ol' Calico.
And there in the whiskey and sawdust,
    I spotted a sweet pain'ted lady for me,
    So, I washed the dust from my dry throat,
    and asked her what she'd like to be.

She told me of plans to find a good man,
    to marry and then settle down.
    She wanted some kids, and a place to call home,
    not too close to town.
There in the dim light and smoke,
    I discovered the answer to this cowboy's prayer,
    a beautiful pain'ted lady,
    clad in green velvet that was worn thread bare.

She danced and twirled, and lit up my world,
    tugging at my heartstrings all the while,
    weaving a magic spell, like Eve did to Adam,
    laced with an angelic smile.
Cupid had sunk his arrow true and deep,
    sparing not one corner of my heart;
    love moved so swiftly,
    like Romeo and Juliet ... we played the part.

There wasn't much spoonin' or courtin' before we wed,
   didn't seem much need;
    on all matters of life and such,
    we almost always agreed.
So, we got us a little spread up north,
   I thought I'd give ranchin' a go;
    she settled in like a good pioneer woman,
    learnin' to cook, stitch and sew.

I started runnin' a few mossy longhorns,
   buildin' a foundation herd,
    and she got her kids … one of each,
    so, it seemed we both had kept our word.
A fine strong lad named Josh,
   in him, I saw more'n just a little-a me,
    and a spittin' image of her mother was our daughter,
    the beautiful Rosalie.

Fightin' Mother Nature's circumstance,
    headstrong we met every test,
    cursin' the drought and prayin' for rain,
    and just hopin' for the best.
We toiled, and sweat, and scraped,
    tryin' to make ends meet,
    always puttin' the youngin's first,
    and tryin' to keep shoe leather on their feet.

But, ranchin's a might tough on a woman,
    especially when winter sets in,
    and long 'bout the tenth year,
    the hope in her eyes was growing dim.
The hard life had cut tracks in her face,
    each line filled with a ghostly glow.
    She just couldn't hang on no more …
    seemed her time had come to go.

I lost her to a fever in the spring,
  she walked through St. Peter's pearly gate,
  and left behind a broken rancher,
  a boy of six ... and a girl of eight.
My sweet painted lady, no longer by my side,
  left my life with no reason,
  and the ranchin' game didn't get any easier,
  with each passin' season.

That summer, I did what was best,
  packed the kids off to a cousin in St. Joe.
  They'd damn shore have a better life,
  and an even chance to learn, and grow.
But, a night never went by without me thinkin'
  of my sweet painted lady before I'd sleep,
  and my kids ... so very far from home,
  filled my dreams, and made me weep.

I tried with all-a my might and worth to keep the ranch,
  but I was all alone.
  The cattle business was dyin' ... just like me,
  and my fingers were raw to the bone.
Then, the blizzard of '86 and the drought of '87,
  wiped the entire herd out,
  and I was left a beaten man,
  where once was a heart, mighty and stout.

The bank took the deed,
  and the cabin where a light of hope once beamed,
  now stood empty and bare,
  'cept for the memories, and things I'd dreamed.
All I had was a string a' horses,
  and a driftin' cowpuncher state of mind,
  so, I shoved south with all a-my gatherin's,
  and left everything else behind.

Driftin' to New Mexico,
    I caught on with the CS outfit, up Cimarron way.
    At least I's workin' cattle,
    and drawin' good cowboy pay.
Charlie Springer ran a tight operation,
    every man dang shore had his worth;
    not a gunsel in the bunch,
    just good puchers, and all salt of the earth.

But, my mind ran wild at night,
    starin' at that bright mountain moon,
    and the wind would whisper in my ear,
    a lonely, mournful tune.
The stars were like her eyes …
    my pain'ted lady haunted me,
    and how I missed young Josh,
    and my darlin' Rosalie.

It's said that time heals all,
    but this I surely doubt,
    for I'm just a shell of a man,
    that's been hollowed and reamed throughout.
I've spent the last ten years on a horse,
    starin' at the south end of a cow,
    and I've come to a sad conclusion that…
    life just passed me by somehow.

I've never questioned topics
    of the good Lord's great design,
    but how my fate's been twisted,
    I consider somewhat less than divine.
I'm not bitter, or angry;
    I just can't seem to understand …
    why God would take my family,
    my cattle, and my land.

My cousin in Missouri,
   who kept my kids as his own,
   stopped writin' me letters,
   when cow camps became my home.
But, the last news I received,
   left me uneasy and depressed;
   it seems my life's one big tragedy,
   to this I will attest.

You see, it seems my son wanted to be a cowboy,
   and follow in his daddy's tracks,
   so he took up gatherin' mustangs,
   drawin' wages from bronco backs.
But, runnin' wild horses is suicide,
   and he took a fatal fall,
   'twas in a boxed in canyon,
   he answered his Master's call.

First my painted lady …
   now Josh had joined her up there,
   to take away my wife and son,
   it all seemed damned unfair.
I felt like I lived a nightmare,
   had God forsaken me?
   But, still I prayed with alla my faith,
   please watch over Rosalie.

We headed to Wyoming,
   for roundup time was here,
   and I spent a month of eatin' dust,
   while ridin' drag in the rear.
We pushed the herd to Cheyenne,
   two thousand head or so,
   and after we penned and loaded,
   I headed for the ol' Calico.

As I swung the big doors open,
    it was like walkin' into a dream,
    a shiver hit my spine,
    as my memory unfolded a forgotten scene.
My sweet pain'ted lady's spirit,
    seemed to dance across the room,
    and I felt an eerie presence,
    that resembled a family tomb.

As my eyes became adjusted,
    to the dim light and the smoke,
    my pain erupted into tears,
    and my hidden feelings awoke.
This was where I met her ...
    some twenty years before,
    and I fell down on my knees,
    upon the sawdust floor.

But, somethin' caught my eye,
    it was a dress of velvet green,
    and a sense of peace engulfed me,
    then I was morbidly serene.
I couldn't see her face,
    as I rose and tried to speak,
    but, everything I'd held inside,
    had made my body limp and weak.

My lips began to tremble,
    I couldn't suffer anymore;
    where once stood a fearless Christian man,
    now lay crumpled on the floor.
She crossed the room to help me,
    it was then that I could see,
    a voice from heaven spoke ...
    "Papa ... it's me ... your darlin' Rosalie!"

Since the inception of the Autry Museum of Western Heritage in Los Angles in 1987, I've had the privilege of being associated with them from the beginning as not only an entertainer, but as a volunteer as well. There are over 40,000 volumes of handwritten diaries and accounts of the old West in their library. This account is a compilation of several different stories that actually happened. I merely assembled them into one story, and even though the piece in its entirety is fiction, each of the events actually occurred at different times, to different people.

Daddy's Saddle

The first memory that comes to mind
    after I laid down my baby rattle,
    was Daddy perchin' me
    high atop his ol' cow horse workin' saddle.
I was shore 'nuff a barnyard buckaroo
    sittin' in that ol' deep dish seat,
    practicin' my cowboy yells for hours
    till Mama hollered for me to come eat.

There was somethin' 'bout that creakin' saddle
    that made music to my ears,
    and the smell-a that worn riggin'
    that testified to all its use and years.
A big high cantle with buckin' rolls
    and double rigged, cowboy style,
    with rounded skirts and hog-nose taps,
    worn from punchin' many a hard mile.

Daddy said Grandpa gave it to him
    just before he retired,
    but he had to earn that family heirloom …
    hard work was required.
So, I knew to lay claim to that saddle,
    I'd have to ride for the brand,
    and put the miles and years in to prove
    I was a worthy hand.

I was pushin' thirty-five,
    when Daddy turned to me one day and said,
    "Take my saddle off the roan ...
    and put it on your post in the tack shed."
A third generation saddle
    inherited with all our family pride,
    made me feel like a barnyard banty rooster,
    yet very humble deep inside.

So, I put my time in that seat
    pushin' cattle, livin' up to the family code;
    it's been my second home for two decades,
    and Lord ... the horses I've rode.
The latigo, billet and cinches
    have been replaced a time or two,
    but it still has that familiar creakin'
    with every dusty mile I do.

So, I put my boy on it
    when he turned five years old,
    and I knew just how he felt
    as his dreams began to unfold.
I told him, "This is my saddle, son,
    and my father's father before him,
    so, if you wanna earn it boy,
    now's the time to begin."

That was quite a few years ago
    and my son just turned thirty-four,
    so, today I gave him that saddle ...
    he earned it ... just like I did before.
He loves it, that goes without sayin',
    and he knows the story that lies within;
    it ain't too hard to find the groove in the seat,
    that was made by three good men.

Now, any puncher would love a good saddle,
    like new, but a hundred years old,
    boy, if leather could talk …
    the stories that could be told.
But every man in my family knows,
    it ain't the saddle that can't be beat;
    it's the quality of the man who owns it,
    that's perched up in the seat.

Chopo

I was visitin' my ol' pard, Mike Martire,
    down in Temeculah one day,
    when I spots this dandy little colt,
    a proud little bay.
Now, Mike's in the thoroughbred business,
    the racin' horse game,
    so, I asked him for the lowdown
    on this colt with no name.

He says, "He's foaled
    from that sweet quarterhorse mare,
    and sired by that black thoroughbred
    standin' over there."
You could get in his stall,
    and he was as gentle as could be;
    he tweren't head-shy or skittish
    from all that I could see.

I liked his disposition,
    and boy could that horse fly!
    He held his head real noble,
    with a keen look in his eye.
I thought he'd make a cow horse,
    judgin' by his conformation and line,
    so, I sized him up, forked over the jack,
    then the colt was mine.

We cut his eggs so he could heal
   in the only home he'd ever known,
   and I tried to picture what he'd be like
   when he came full grown.
Two socks in the rear,
   and a star blazed on his head,
   with the kindness of a quarterhorse,
   and courage of a thoroughbred.

I told Mike I'd pick him up later,
   when I had time to spare,
   and then searched my mind
   for the name that he'd bear.
I recalled an ol' song by Jack Thorp,
   a good one I know,
   'bout a steady, faithful cow horse
   by the name of ... Chopo.

Now, I'm not much on hot bloods;
   I like a trusty quarterhorse,
   but, there's always an exception
   to every rule, a-course,
And breakin' horses is a job
   that's a full time deal,
   but, I thought for ol' Chopo,
   I had a sixth sense I could feel.

I went to pick him up one day,
   but a trailer he'd never seen,
   and he didn't exactly take to it,
   like any horse that's green.
Now, guys like Parelli or Hunt,
   they might teach to load in one try,
   but, most of us end up a-cussin' and a-fightin',
   till the nag's 'bout to die.

So, we aced him up with two cc's,
   till his tool box was droopin' down,
   he was so juiced up on Rompun,
   his ol' head 'bout hit the ground.
With a butt rope tightly wrapped,
   and one 'round his poll,
   we figgered to just ease this horse
   in the trailer before he tried to roll.

But, then he came alive,
   just like he'd never had a shot,
   and three of us was a-hangin' on for dear life,
   with everything we got!
He reared, and fought for hours,
   lathered up from head to tail,
   and broke two ropes, and burned our hides,
   in his effort to prevail.

He went down twice,
   I loosed the rope so he wouldn't choke;
   both times he sprang up
   even madder, just goin' for broke!
But, finally he was humiliated,
   and calmly stepped right in,
   well, at least he proved he had spirit,
   and an attitude to win.

I won the fight, and hauled him home,
    and opened the trailer door;
      I gently tried to coax him out,
      but this he chose to ignore.
So, I backed the trailer up to the corral
    to avoid another fight,
      and he stepped out on his own …
      sometime late that night!

Ol' Chopo had some spunk,
    but now the trainin' had to begin,
      so, I ran his butt ragged,
      crackin' him out in the round pen.
His first few saddles went purty smooth,
    and I was actually surprised,
      which sorta proved he had the makin's,
      just as I had surmised.

He was a good people horse,
    and had the strength of a brute,
      more scared of hisself than me,
      and a clumsy ol' galoot.
But, he started movin' a little smoother
    in the arena that spring,
      doin' nice figure eights,
      and to the rail he'd cling.

He'd been trimmed now and then,
    but the time had come to be shod,
      and rememberin' the trailer incident,
      I knew I'd have to fight the clod.
Now, a first shoein' can be aided
    with the help of stud chain,
      but, not ol' Chopo …
      he wasn't even phased by the pain.

So, we twitched up his lip,
    hopin' to numb the ol' steed,
    but, he kept a-rearin' and a-fightin',
    like any hot blood breed!
He calmed down a little,
    after his ribs took a size 10 THUMP,
    and a horse shoein' rasp
    sternly laid 'cross his big ol' rump!

So, the time finally came,
    in the pasture I thought we'd go,
    but, it didn't take long
    for ol' Chopo to decide to blow!
He was dancin' in little circles,
    wound tighter'n a two dollar watch;
    he was crow hoppin' and a-jiggin',
    and a-beatin' up my crotch!

We was workin' some hills,
    and he was scared half to death,
    but, I eased him through the paces,
    and just tried to hold my breath!
Then he stepped off one backwards,
    I couldn't turn his head 'round,
    that feather-head and me separated,
    and I kissed the rocky ground!

'Twas a twenty foot drop,
    and how he survived I'll never know,
    but, he shore 'nuff learned a lot that day,
    at the cost of all my woe!
I broke a finger bailin' off,
    and laid another open to the bone,
    but, my pride was intact,
    for at least I wasn't thrown.

So, while I healed up,
    I gave him to Jason Jacobs to ride for awhile,
    'cause he just needed to be rode a lot,
    to sharpen up his style.
Now, Jace knows his horses,
    fact is, he's a top hand,
    so, when he agreed to ride Chopo,
    I wondered what he'd planned.

I picked him up a month later,
    but he was bandaged 'round the hocks,
    the idiot had backed over a wheelbarrow,
    and tangled with a mail box!
So, I asked Jace what he'd taught him,
    as I checked his cut up rear,
    he said, "I taught him to heal a cut,
    he's been that way since you left him here!"

Now, these runnin' quarters are built for speed,
    what a lengthy gait,
      so, I'd run ol' Chopo 'cross the hills
      to develop this inbred trait.
He'd move along so swiftly, man,
    that horse shore had some nerve;
      occasionally, he'd spook, and try to dump me
      while roundin' out a curve.

He still had one bad habit …
    runnin' backwards when he was scared,
      but, I just bailed off and watched the wreck,
      to let him learn from what he dared!
I'd let a few hands ride him,
    but only those I could trust,
      'cause he was more'n a handful,
      to be an expert was a must!

It got to be a joke 'round the ranch
    the cowboys attitudes were perverse
      'bout this big ol' bay with great potential,
      that loved to run just in reverse!
So, I brought him along slow,
    he'd go weeks without a flaw,
      but, then he'd forget which way he was goin',
      and run backwards down in a draw!

Like the time we rode with Wayne Walston,
    and his unruly buckskin mare,
      that danced and pranced 'cross the hills
      and reared up in the air.
She got ol' Chopo nervous,
    her every move he did reflect,
      and I knew it wouldn't be long
      before me and him would disconnect!

I'd gotten purty good at bailin' off,
    so through the air I flew,
    and landed upright like Hawkeye Henson,
    as I bid ol' Chopo adieu!
He ran full speed backwards,
    and took his usual fall,
    and crash-landed in a dusty heap,
    against the canyon wall!

Now, when he got like that,
    I's in a fix without a clue,
    reinin' up to stop runnin' backwards,
    sure ain't what to do!
I could dig my spurs into his hide,
    but all to no avail;
    he'd just pick up his gait,
    and keep runnin' backwards down the trail.

But, I figgered I'd start team pennin'
    to get his mind in a bovine direction,
    'cause, after all, to rope off of him
    was my final goal projection.
Now, he'd been 'round cattle before,
    but never in the same pen,
    so, those of us who knew the horse,
    waited for the fun to begin!

Shore 'nuff, he whirled 'round,
   and then he proudly scat,
     but I'll be durned if we didn't pen three steers,
     in twenty seconds flat!
It finally dawned upon me,
   that one eventful day,
     he just feels more comfortable ...
     runnin' the opposite way!

At first what I thought was loco,
   or maybe a dyslexic mind,
     could be a freak of nature, possibly ...
     an eyeball in his behind!
Now, you might scoff at my story,
   or think it can't be true,
     but I swear to God he's different
     from any horse you ever knew!

So, I worked him for a year,
   in the direction he liked the best,
     and now to see his unusual style,
     well, you've got to be impressed!
I've had to make some adjustments,
   of how I sit upon his back,
     and slightly rearrange my saddle riggin',
     and all my ropin' tack!

I put my hat on backwards,
   and spurs upon my toes,
     and kick him in the shoulders,
     and pull the reins up hard to go!
Turnin's all done the opposite,
   but to whoa is kinda strange,
     'cause when it's time to stop ...
     I just let go-a my reins!

He ropes purty good now,
    but one thing we never overcame,
    and that's to get cowboys at jackpots,
    to change the rules of the game!
'Cause I start at the end of the arena,
    and run backwards on the fly,
    and try to rope two in the air,
    of a steer that's streakin' by!

So, I don't get many pardners,
    and for ol' Chopo it's a shame,
    he dang shore had the makin's,
    so I guess I'll take the blame.
He might be slightly different,
    but it's my fault we don't win a purse,
    'cause you can't team rope with a pardner,
    whose horse runs just in reverse!

Beauty and the Bees

It was a bright, clean day and quite sunny outside,
    and it seemed only natural to saddle up for a ride.
The ponies were all frisky, with spring in the air,
    so, I tacked up the bay, and the buckskin mare.

There was me and ol' Jim, who's a farrier by trade,
    a gal that I knew, and a new friend she'd just made.
The gal's name was Sally, and she said she rode quite well,
    so, I put her on the buckskin, hopin' she wouldn't give her hell!

Sally was a fair-haired beauty, with tan skin all aglow,
    and a soft silky voice that melted Jim when she said, "*Hello.*"
She knew what she was doin' all right, she sat a real good seat,
    so, we loped down the road atop high-steppin' feet.

I figgered we'd do a four hour loop, it seemed a perfect day,
    with sage a-bloomin' purple in the late part of May.
We'd peel down into Charlie Canyon, my plan was complete,
    but, ridin' in that country, you never know what you'll meet.

Well, the canyon was alive with wildlife skitterin' to and fro,
    and all the spring wildflowers, with new cholla in full grow.
The horses were sure broncy, but everyone was doin' all right,
    we were just frolickin' through the canyon in the May sunlight.

As we rode toward the peak to drop down into the draw,
    my eyes encountered a sight the likes I never saw!
There were hundreds of honey bee hives, smack in our path,
    and there really wasn't any way to escape the oncoming wrath!

"Put the iron to your horse," I yelled, "ain't no turnin' back!
    Swat the bees from your eyes and grab a-hold of your kack!"
So, we broke to a run, firmly set in our mind,
    with a million mad bees closin' in from behind!

Well, they caught me first, my horse took one in the eye,
    but, they abandoned my hide and continued to fly!
The gal that was with me took nary a sting,
    and I kinda wondered what their next move would bring!

Jim took a couple, but he swatted 'em with his hat,
    so, he fared okay in his hand-to-hand combat!
Now, with three of us safe, we were able to see,
    what the boilin' fury of the swarm was to be!

They hit Sally purty hard, I'd say … a thousand or so,
    then the buckskin figgered it was time to really blow!
They shot over the rise … the beauty and the mare,
    with that whole swarm of bees all in her hair!

We caught her in a mile, 'neath the grove of some trees,
    she had her hands full, fightin' the mare and the bees!
The horse was a-rearin' and lookin' to wreck,
    with all them hungry bees stingin' the back of her neck!

Jim caught the mare, and I jerked Sally from the saddle,
    so, now we had ourselves two separate battles!
We all kept a-swingin' and chased away the bees,
    and the fair-haired beauty collapsed to her knees!

We pulled out the stingers from her head to her toes,
    and scraped the dead bees from offa her clothes.
I gotta hand to Sally, she toughed it out alright,
    but, I must admit … she shore was a sight!

Arrivin' back home, we gave her a steak and a tub,
   a clean pair of clothes and an alcohol rub.
She stayed quite sore, and I'm sure would feel,
   she'd NEVER forget that day of the honey bee ordeal!

So, the moral here is simple you see,
   if you ever encounter a swarm of mad bees,
make shore your ridin' pardners aren't crazy as a loon,
   to let you go trail ridin' in spring ...
   WEARIN' HONEYSUCKLE PERFUME!

෩   ෨

Fortunately, Sally was real handy with a horse, and
managed to stay in the saddle until the rescue, or we
woulda had a first class wreck.

One Thing or Another

There's one thing we'll all agree on,
    of this I have no doubt.
    When in Hell is this gonna end,
    this plague we call the drought?
It's parched our grazin' land
    and burned up all the hay,
    but the almanac says it'll be over soon …
    maybe even today!

The farmers say, it's a sun-spot cycle
    that happens every seven years,
    but, lookin' at them skinny cattle,
    I'm expectin' my worst fears.
Some of the outfits sold out …
    shortly after they went insane,
    wasn't no sense in hangin' on no more …
    just *prayin'* for rain.

HEY! Look at them storm clouds,
    and is that thunder that I hear?
    Oh, thank you Dear Lord,
    now I think I'll make it through the year!
Well, the land is quenched,
    and we've all had a long, cool drink,
    the seed's startin' to sprout
    and soon we'll be in the pink!

Them cattle are sure gettin' fat,
 and that makes me mighty glad,
 there's bunch-grass belly high
 with all this rain that we've had.
Well, I reckon I'll start cleanin' up
 all this mess from the flood,
 damned this crazy weather ....
 now, I'm knee-deep in mud!

All the deer trails are washed out,
 ain't safe for cattle now;
 reckon I'll clear that canyon
 with some sweat, mule and plow.
These blasted rattlesnakes are takin' over,
 with all this new growed brush,
 every bean field's getting' boggy,
 and my horses all have thrush!

The water gaps need cleanin',
 and the barn roof's got a leak;
 if it ever dries out again I'll fix it,
 maybe sometime next week!
There's mold on all the saddles,
 and my hay is ruined and wet,
 and I've dug my pickup outta the ditch
 for the last time you can bet!

There's a hole in my slicker ...
  wouldn't you know it ... just my luck.
  It's a wonder I don't grow wings and fly,
  'cause I'm livin' like a duck!
I've 'bout had it up to here,
  with all this rain I can do without,
  and I never thought I'd say it ...
  but, I sure do miss the drought!

But, so it goes with Mother Nature,
  that's why you'll hear ranchers say,
  "If it ain't one thing or another ...
  then it's somethin' else on the way!"

❧　❧

The drought that started in California in 1985, finally broke in 1991. When it did, it broke with a vengeance, and we went from one extreme to another.

Chewin' Tobacco

I took this gal out,
    and friends, I mean to say,
    she wasn't exactly well-versed
    in the 'cowboy way.'
Now, she'd always seen me
    with this big ol' plug a-chaw,
    a knot the size of a golf ball,
    stuck right here in my jaw.

I told her, "Yep, it's somethin'
    a lot of cowboys do,
    instead of smokin, well,
    it's a little more convenient to chew."
So, she figgers to fit in,
    and to be no slouch,
    she'd go out ta buy her
    some Beechnut Tobacco, in a pouch.

Well, she loaded up purty heavy,
    and gave this wispy little grin,
    then she swallered real hard,
    and her eyes began to spin!
She says, "I'm feelin' a little faint,
    I must be getting' the flu!"
    I said, "No darlin, it's from all that tobacco
    you're tryin' to chew."

She says, "No ... no ... I mean it's like a fever,
    and man is it gettin' hot?"
    I said, "Yep, it's from all that
    durn chewin' tobacco that you got."
She says, "No ... I mean I'm queezy ...
    and I think I'm gonna get sick!"
    I said, "I know, hon, I reckon you better find you
    a bathroom purty quick!"

Well, she was gone for 'bout an hour,
    and finally she returned,
    but she was blue ... all 'round her edges ...
    and a valuable lesson she'd learned.
She bemoans the fact
    that we cowboys are such as hearty lot,
    but as far as the art of chewin' tobacco ...
    well, she'd just rather not!

I said, "Well, I appreciate the fact
    you hold us waddies in such high esteem,
    but, I figger on one point ... well ...
    it's best I come clean.
You see, it's really nice you think
    we cowboys are all quite so dandy,
    but, I reckon I shoulda told you, hon ...
    I been chewin' licorice candy!"

Retirement

Come here, ol' fella,
    let's me and you have a little chat.
    I think I'm gonna turn you loose ...
    what do you think about that?
You see, you been 'bout as steady
    as any horse ever could,
    and you done every thing I ever asked you ...
    just like you should.

You've carried me many a mile,
    and hardly ever did anything wrong,
    why, you even stood still while
    I was a-howlin my night herd song.
I never seen you pin your ears in anger,
    or even roll a mean eye,
    you were always up for the task,
    and dang shore had more than 'nuff try.

Why, even when you was a little colt,
    you always seemed to know just what to do,
    and I reckon them coupla spankin's
    turned out to be purty good for you.
We been in a passel a fixes,
    and you weren't never the one to blame,
    but you got me through my mistakes,
    and never even came up lame.

We've worked some purty rough country,
    and your ol hide's shore been nicked,
    and for gluin' yourself to a set a-hocks,
    all you ever got was ... cow kicked.
Some a them hot dry summers,
    you even went on one day's rest,
    and knee deep in snow, or mud,
    well ... by golly, you always done your best.

You've carried new born calves ... and kids
    ... panniers and blocks of salt,
    and I can't recall that any one of your wrecks
    was ever even your fault.
But, after twenty years of hard work,
    and ridin' this fence line wire,
    well, I reckon it's time
    I pulled your shoes ... and let you retire.

Hey, I'll come pull you out
    for a gather now and then,
    and don't worry ol' pard,
    you ain't gonna be cooped up in no pen.
Just go out and enjoy yourself,
    and eat that bunchgrass belly high.
    It's your long overdue reward, my friend,
    and well, I ain't sayin' good-bye.

I know ol' fella ...
    don't look at me that-a-way.
    I want you to listen,
    and understand what I'm tryin' to say...
that you've earned your keep ...
    so go out in that pasture and race around,
    maybe you can show them young horses out there
    how to hold their ground ...

'Cause your job ain't over fella …
    it's just gonna go through a little change,
    it's time you showed them little colts out there
    the workin's of a cattle range.
They'll understand you … just sorta let 'em know
    how they're supposed to be,
    you know what to do ol' bud …
    look how you took care a-me.

Well, thanks for the chat ol' fella …
    and I know you understand …
    I'm right proud to have seen you work so hard,
    ridin' for this brand.
Come on down and visit me …
    I'll meet you back there at the north fence …
    you're 'bout the only one I can talk to 'round here
    that even makes any sense.

I know things are gonna be a little different for you,
    but like always, I'm sure you'll adjust;
    I need you more'n ever now …
    and I know you … by God … I can trust.
Oh, one last thing, *amigo* …
    in you I must confide …
    you been the best, ol' pard …
    adios … and thanks for the ride.

                ও ও

    I remember an old saying when I was growin' up … 'you might know three good women before you're laid down dead, and MAYBE … just MAYBE … ride three good horses for every hundred head.' The good ones are rare, indeed.

My Ol' Pard Les

It's true I confess, my ol' pard Les,
 Is 'bout the best friend I ever had.
He takes my best shot, and I kid him a lot,
 'bout bein' my dear ol' dad.

His life it portrays, of a cowboy's ways,
 a student of the great American West.
His mold is from a cast of better days long past,
 and by God he's learned from the best.

When the goin' get rough, there ain't nothin' too tough,
 he's a hand and a top buckaroo.
He don't savvy quit, when it takes muscle and spit,
 and to ride the river with, well, he'll do.

When all's said and done, we've shore had some fun,
 and I don't think I've ever seen him mad.
Well, there ain't no doubt, he's shore helped me out,
 helpin' me bust some of my rank horses that are bad.

I keep my eye peeled out, 'cause there ain' no doubt,
 that sometimes he don't eat like he should.
So, I take him beans by the pot, and my chili that's too hot,
 and some of the wife's homemade bread that's shore 'nuff good.

We do a few shows, recitin' our prose,
 and a finer poet I've never heard.
His life's fulla stories, some funny, some gory,
 and he shore has a way with a spoken word.

He's not much on geography, but shore knows cowography,
   and a hundred ways to fix an ol' gate.
At doctorin' sick steers, well, he has no peer,
   but he's always runnin' a tad late.

He's nice to his sister, he's a bronc peelin' twister,
   and I've never seen him be short or mean.
At my weddin' that year, he stood by me so near,
   and for the occasion even bought a pair of new jeans.

I remember last winter, he chopped into splinter,
   enough firewood to last me through May.
He helps me work on my truck, when I've run out of patience and luck,
   'cause mechanicin's 'bout his best fortay.

So, I've immortalized you in verse, but what's even worse,
   is I've made you sound like a God-given saint.
But, it ain't too hard, 'cause, I'll tell you ol' pard,
   you're 'bout as steady as my good ol' paint.

But, you got one flaw, and now I'm layin' down the law,
   so, I want you listen up keen.
Don't make me get tough, but enough is enough,
   can I *PLEASE* have back my "Cowboy" magazine!!!

                                                                       ~∂⁓ ∾⁓

For as long as Les Buffham and I have known each other, I reckon we've earned the right to heckle one another. For some time, I did razz him a lot 'bout bein' my dad, but since then I've grayed 'round the edges some, have put on a little weight, and am wearin' bifocals, I now concede to the fact that he's like an older brother ... one that's *much older*!

The Quake of '94

It was January, year '94,
    when the earth began to shake,
    a nightmare spawned by the devil himself,
    in the form of a deadly earthquake.

As I lay there in peaceful slumber,
    Mother Nature awakened first,
    for Hell's account was overdrawn ...
    from her bowels Satan burst.

It started as a gentle rumble,
    then unending waves of roar,
    with brutal violence it shook me awake,
    in the dark at half past four.

I covered my woman with my body,
    and we both started to scream,
    as the earth belched out its message,
    that this was more than a bad dream.

The walls came crashing down,
    moving things the weight of a dozen men,
    spitting objects all around us,
    then heaving them across the room again.

I fumbled for my clothes in the dark,
    but all I found was broken glass,
    and then I began to wonder ...
    how long the damned thing would last.

Another tremor quickly followed,
 as I scrambled to find a light,
 and upstairs my woman still screamed,
 gripped by sheer terror and morbid fright.

It took thirty minutes to get dressed,
 stepping over things we used to own,
 then you start worryin' 'bout your family,
 but you realize ... there ain't no phone.

We evacuated the dusty building,
 and took refuge in the truck,
 swarms of aftershocks were cruel,
 and we felt sure we'd run out of luck.

At first, I thought it was our own private Hell,
 till the dark gave way to light,
 then I saw all the mass devastation,
 and the panic of the homeless in flight.

We gathered up some basics,
 and left most everything we owned,
 knowin' we'd have to come back later,
 to what used to be a home.

Our nerves were worn and frazzled,
 and our bodies begged for sleep,
 but the quake was our "boogeyman" ...
 that left our life in a crumbled heap.

Now, I've been through a few shakers,
 and some were boilin' mean,
 but, this was more evil than a tremor ...
 it's the worst I'd ever seen.

Unknowingly, we always picture Mother Nature
    as something placid and serene,
    like powdered snow upon the mountain,
    or a gentle rain that washes clean.

But, this night of wrath and fury,
    had no feeling of mortal emotion,
    as it struck fear in the hearts of everyone,
    with it's deafening destructive motion.

But, we went back to face disaster,
    although it's what we wanted to do the least,
    because Satan will always be lurking,
    in the hot belly of the beast.

I'm sure we'll make it through all right,
    because God is on our side,
    and we've got a lot more livin' to do,
    so, we won't be detoured or denied.

We'll just keep praying, and count our blessings,
    for years and many, many more,
    of how God mercifully spared our lives …
    in the quake of '94.

    Ironically, we had a trip planned to go check out New Mexico five days after the earthquake anyway. Our plan had been to move in the summer, not January. However, after we went to New Mexico, we decided to move right away, instead of waiting. Most everything we owned was destroyed, except our horses, so we sold them, salvaged and stored what we could, and left. This wasn't exactly the way we wanted to relocate, but God does things according to his plan, not ours, so we started over.

Cowboy Bill and Booker T.

I got a good friend named Bill King,
    who ranches in Los Alamos high on a hill.
He's a happy sort fella and native Californio,
    and we simply call him ... Cowboy Bill.

Now, Cowboy Bill, like most big ranchers,
    seems to have a dog or two.
At best, they help gather cattle,
    but a lot of 'em don't know what the Hell to do.

Bill had one such lunkhead on the ranch,
    who was as stubborn as could be.
A little ol' black Heinz 57 mutt,
    and his name was ... Booker T.

Booker was a real jock who kinda smiled,
    and always tried to please his master.
But, he was one brick short of a full load,
    and constantly courted disaster.

Booker never had a kind word spoken to him,
    'cause he was always in the wrong place.
But, that dog NEVER quit tryin'
    to put a smile on ol' Bill's face.

All the kids loved Booker T.,
    and he didn't even chase the cat.
But, when it came to workin' cattle,
    he never knew where he's supposed to be at.

One winter, Bill decides to go huntin',
    to see if he could bag him a big ol' buck deer,
and feelin' kinda sorry for the ol' potlicker,
    said, "Come on Booker … get on in here!"

They struck off for the high country,
    and ol' Booker T.'s a-ridin' in the back.
Cowboy Bill had visions a-dancin' in his head
    of bringin' home a twelve point rack.

Bill fashioned up some cover,
    and perched hisself high up a tree.
Him and that ol' dog began a-waitin',
    just as patient as could be.

Cowboy Bill spies a rogue buck,
    and squeezed a shot off for the kill.
But, he only winged the giant white tail,
    and he disappeared 'cross a hill.

Ol' Bill sets off a-trackin' blood,
    with Booker T. there close behind.
But, that crazy canine goes off a-chasin' rabbits,
    so Bill hollers, "Booker … we got a deer to find!"

Cowboy Bill's prowess as a tracker
   soon began to fail.
So, he beckons to Booker T. ,
   "Go get 'em boy ... get that ol' white tail!"

Well, the brush began to poppin',
   as Booker crashed through the oaks and pine.
He's a-howlin' like a thirsty bloodhound,
   and he left Cowboy Bill far behind.

Bill followed the yelping bungler for a mile,
   then the brush began to clear,
and I'll be durned if ol' Booker hadn't succeeded
   in bayin' up that crippled deer.

Bill put the buck out of his misery,
   and ol' Booker's 'bout to come unglued,
'cause that mutt *FINALLY* did somethin' right,
   and he shore saw a change in his master's mood.

Bill says, "Atta boy Booker ... good dog!"
   as he gutted the big buck deer.
Booker T.'s a-twirlin' 'round in circles,
   feelin' like he has no other peer.

Cowboy Bill's plumb agog,
   figgerin' that dog shore had a streak a good luck.
He packed out his wall-sized trophy,
   and said, "Go on Booker ... go get in the truck!"

Well, that dog was so excited
   'bout fillin' his master up with glee,
he jumped clean over the pickup bed
   and knocked hisself out cold on a tree!

Bill tied the deer to the left fender,
    and strapped Booker to the one on the right.
He hauled 'em both home to the ranch,
    tied to the truck there real tight.

Booker T. finally came 'round
    from knockin' hisself unconscious and dumb,
and he got a big ol' hunka venison flank,
    for a fearless job, well done.

Now, when dogs and horses pass on
    to cross the great divide way up yonder,
their feats of daring courage are magnified,
    as their owners memories grow fonder.

Today, if you ask Cowboy Bill 'bout Booker T.,
    that ol' black dog that was the litter's runt,
he'll tell you, "He couldn't work cattle … or even get in the truck …
    but boy he shore could hunt!"

❧ ❧

    Bill King is one of those rare people who has a treasure
chest full of stories. The strangest things seem to happen to
him, and what's more amazing, most of 'em are true. He's
always at Elko every year, and if you run into him at one of
the jam sessions, ask him to sing you "Waltz Across Texas,"
or tell you 'bout the time he lost his hat while singin' the
national anthem at the Salinas Rodeo.

Thinkin' It Over

I don't wanna be no cowboy,
    I've 'bout had it up to here.
It ain't all it's pumped up to be,
    bein' a babysitter for a steer.

I'm tired of rope burns on my hands,
    and cockleburrs in my durn bed.
There's duct tape holdin' my boots together,
    and a dull achin' in my head.

I've had my fill acold, wet mornin's,
    with a slicker that don't even keep me dry.
And I've consumed enough dang beans
    to make a dozen men beg to die.

I don't ever want the jigger boss
    to rope another rank horse for me to ride.
Just so I can pick out thorns from my leggin's
    that are buried deep in my hide.

I'm sick and tired of ridin' with Willie
    and his smelly ol' buzzard breath.
His night singin' drives me crazy,
    and his conversation just bores me to death.

The chuck on this outfit's the worst …
    'cause no recipes were ever learned.
The coffee tastes like pine tar …
    and the sourdough's always burned.

I don't ever wanna see another inch of barbed wire,
   or even a pair of fencin' pliers.
I've 'bout had enough of poundin' steeples,
   and all them hotshots the foreman hires.

I'll be danged if I ever dig one more water box …
   or nurse a prolapsed cow.
And why even fix them broken fence posts
   when they end up breakin' again, anyhow?

I think I'll move to town and work …
   I reckon I could do purty well.
I'll quit this romantic cowboy life
   and this ranch can go straight to Hell.

Shoot, I could be … a welder …
   I've done a little in my day.
But, that work's too durn hot for me,
   no matter what the pay.

Or, maybe I could … drive a rig …
   though it's really not my style.
I think I'd much rather be a-horseback
   if I'm travelin' by the mile.

But, I could be … a mechanic …
   even though I hate twistin' a wrench.
Besides, them garages are dark and dingy,
   and they possess an oily stench.

I bet I could do some kinda sales,
   well … maybe … if I really tried.
But I don't think I could spend that much time
   bein' cooped up inside.

I reckon punchin' cows is somethin'
    that really ain't all that bad.
And that jigger boss might be 'onry,
    but he's still the best one I ever had.

The food out here will always stink,
    and I'm sure that'll never change.
But, I reckon it'll fill my empty hole
    when I'm out here on the range.

"HEY WILLIE … come over here, pard,
    and tell me how you're gettin' along.
I'll pull night guard for you next week,
    so I won't have to hear that Gawd-awful song!"

I reckon I'll hit the feathers,
    and knock the stickers outta my roll.
There's a heap a-fencin' to do tomorrow …
    and I believe that mare's gonna foal.

So, I guess I'll keep a-punchin' cows …
    givin' it some thought it's plain to see …
it might not be easy bein' a cowboy …
    but there's nothin' else I'd rather be.

I reckon some who draw a wage a-horseback, livin' a
cowboy life, have this thought cross their mind, and some
don't. Fact is, those who think about quittin', usually
realize, sooner or later, that it's a real hard thing to give up.
Those who never consider quittin' are lucky 'cause they
never have to confront that gut-wrenching, heart-breaking
decision.

Cow Camp Buckaroo

There's things the BLM and ranchers agree on,
    though they're few and far between,
    like the advantage of big outfits havin' line camps,
    to keep the land pure and clean.

Now, the rancher will tell you a line camp
    helps his calves weaning weight get raised.
    He can improve the condition of his allotments,
    and control the pattern where his cattle's grazed.

Though both rancher and BLM reps
    seem to like the idea of a line camp shack,
    they ain't the one stuck out there a-livin'
    where a four wheeler stops its tracks.

A fella can getta might lonesome out there
    with nary a soul around.
    Some stories recall grisly accounts
    of cowpokes that weren't never found.

You don't have to be no top-notch buckaroo
    'cause the work really ain't all that hard,
    but, you best be good company for yourself
    'cause a mirror's your only pard.

Nine outta ten cowboys would give anything
    to have a job where the boss ain't breathin' down your neck,
    but, ninety-nine outta hundred a-those would crack,
    ridin' out one full winter for their check.

That kinda solitude punches holes in your character,
    and creates a mental strain.
    It's sorta like a paranoid stir crazy,
    that gobbles up your brain.

There ain't no radio, or satellite dish,
    or even a phone to talk into;
    so, to break up the monotony a little,
    you best have a dog or two.

It's mostly choppin' ice, and ridin' fence,
    or doctorin' steers when there's a need,
    servicin' windmills, or scatterin' bulls,
    and bringin' the weak stock in for feed.

Sometimes, there's late calves to mark,
    and watchin' water holes dry up.
    Then, you chop more ice, and ride fence again,
    and play some with your pup.

The first month ain't too bad it seems,
    you get up early and start a fire.
    Then, you cook up a big ol' breakfast,
    before you ride the fence line wire.

You ride a big circle, and go explorin',
    and rope a yearlin' just for fun,
    fix a nice hearty supper, then wash the dishes,
    and shave with the rinse water when you're done.

Once a week, you simmer a pot of beans,
    or maybe labor over a stew.
    If someone stumbles onto your camp,
    you stay in the bushes outta view.

But, the second month things start a-changin',
   with nothin' left to explore,
   no breakfast anymore … just coffee,
   and sight seein' ain't fun no more.

You don't rope that yearlin' just for the heck of it,
   not since you lost your good rope.
   You start eatin' leftovers in the evenin',
   and wash the dishes twice a week, with no soap.

You quit shavin' with regularity,
   and don't fix no beans or stew.
   Kinda senseless tryin' to keep things tidy,
   when there ain't no one there but you.

The third and fourth month things worsen,
   as you turn into some sorta hermit man.
   You eat whatever's handy,
   and heat it up right in the can.

The dishes lie in soak for weeks,
   so you wipe a fork off with the tail of your shirt.
   Somehow, you reason in your boggled mind,
   that, yeah, it's dirty … but it's clean dirt!

You don't shave till you're a-itchin',
   and you've read everything through and through,
   you start talkin' to your horses … a lot,
   and they start talkin' back to you!

You plumb wore out your decka cards playin' solitaire,
   and you shore do sleep a lot.
   But, you did solve all the world's problems,
   and figgered out how to make money by the pot!

By the end of the season, you've got a full beard,
    and your eyes are sunk back in your head.
    You've lost 'bout thirty pounds,
    and you start wonderin' if you're dead!

Your jeans are a-sheddin' water,
    from the greasy dirt and all the blood,
    and you start ridin' closer to the road,
    hopin' someone'll get stuck in the mud!

If you do happen upon a wayward stranger,
    you start babblin' like a durn fool.
    They all think your kinda weird,
    'cause now you're talkin' like your mule!

You've cultivated endless hobbies,
    besides braidin' rawhide and hitchin' hair.
    Now, you collect deer antlers and pine cones,
    and can stack match sticks a foot in the air!

You've been infected with cowboy insanity,
    and you're crazy as a durn loon.
    But, with some decent conversation and home cookin',
    You might recover ... sometime in June!

But, if you remain in this frenzied state,
    for ... say, more'n a month or two,
    you best take that same job next winter,
    'cause a line camp's the only place for you!

But, as for me, well, I've had my fill,
    no more of that life without a care.
    It sure is a nice place to visit ...
    but I don't think I wanna live there!

❧   ❧

Personally, I've never spent more'n one night in a line camp. My good friend, Mackey Hedges, spent some twenty five years livin' in line camps. His middle son, Jed, was six years old before he ever even turned on an electric light switch. Many of his experiences of camp life were jotted down by his wife, Candice, and published in an article in *Western Horseman*, and that's where the inspiration for this poem comes from.

So, You Wanna Be a Cowboy Poet?

A few privileged souls live the life of a cowboy,
    dyed in the wool, and their hands dang shore show it.
But let me enlighten you to the pitfalls and merits,
    of bein' a cowboy poet.

Folks think it's glamorous and rewarding,
    havin' all a-them books and tapes for sale.
If they only knew how much time you spend
    tryin' to track down your last month's mail.

We've all had to give up doin' ranch work,
    Ain't no time left for punchin' cows no more.
Some of us don't see home for weeks,
    but I know we're still cowboys 'cause we're poor.

Most of us spend our days in airplanes,
    or pickups and buses, just commutin',
sleepin' sittin' up on some livin' room couch,
    not in hotels all highfalutin.

Oh, we get a fee, and revenue from our concessions,
    so don't let me steer you wrong.
But, after overhead, and miscellaneous expenses,
    we drop the rest in the juke for a song.

So, at best it's a break-even kinda deal,
    and a business that don't cut you no slack.
Some do better than others, like that fella …
    what's his name? … oh yeah, Baxter Black.

Sometimes you go to pull out a business card
    from your ol' briefcase that never locks,
when out pops a bull calf nut sack someone gave you,
    wrapped up in a pair of dirty socks.

You eat a lot at greasy spoon cafes,
    and the food at county fairs is all the same.
You get to where you don't ever wanna see potato salad again,
    and the chili's always too bland and tame.

But, if you think it's hard on me or my cronies,
    livin' this kinda unsettled life,
well, my friend, let me tell you what it's like
    bein' a cowboy poet's WIFE.

It's always, "Hon, wash me out a shirt and iron it,
    and go gas up the truck if you get a chance.
Pick me up a roll a snoose, and some jerky,
    and put a new crease in my good pants."

She feels lucky when she sees you every other week,
    and she knows it don't do no good to gripe.
But, you take her with you, now and then,
    'cause when you write somethin' new she can type.

Oh, I know it sounds kinda chauvinistic,
    and man, can she throw you some dirty looks.
But, I get too busy BS'n with my buddies,
    somebody's gotta sell the tapes and books.

So, you wonder why guys like me do it,
    puttin' all the hard miles in doin' these shows?
Well, it ain't for the fame or the glory,
    or for the profit sharing plan, God only knows!

It's so we can put a smile on your face,
    or maybe see you reach for a belly laugh that's deep.
Sometimes, we just wanna make you ponder,
    or forget your troubles that are piled in a heap.

We wanna make you think 'bout your heritage,
    and talk 'bout our endangered ranchin' tradition.
We want you to enjoy visitin' with your friends,
    and discuss the fate of the cowboys' present condition.

So, in conclusion … if you've ever been a cowboy,
    or you just wanna put your ranch up for sale,
maybe, you might wanna hit the poetry circuit,
    and sing a song, or spin a rhyme, or just tell a tale.

Bring along your wife, 'cause she's worth it,
    after all, she married you for better or for worse,
and put down your memories of your cowboy life,
    in rhyme, rhythm, song and verse.

You won't spend as much time a-horseback,
    but that warm feelin' inside … well, you'll know it.
It shore is worth it, chattin' with folks like ya-ll,
    when you become a cowboy poet.

Hey Grandpa

Hey Grandpa, let's go down to the barn and do some ropin',
   maybe you can help me out ... at least that's what I'm hopin'.
I don't know what I'm doin' wrong, or why it seems so hard,
   I seem to do okay Grandpa ... when I'm ropin' in the yard.

Don't worry son, you ain't been ropin' all that long,
   build you a loop and let's see what you might be doin' wrong.
You know, you're still knee high to a button, so don't expect too much,
   there's a lot to this ropin' deal; it takes a special kinda touch.

Hey Grandpa, maybe I need a scant rope, or maybe a softer lay,
   I was usin' one of Dad's ol' 7/16 ropes the other day,
and you know, it felt real good, but it sure was awful big,
   you shoulda seen me rope and stretch out Grandma-s pig!

You better watch your step, boy, and stick to catchin' cattle,
   if Grandma catches you, you're gonna have yourself quite a battle.
Now, you keep that 3/8, and rope that dummy a hundred loops a day,
   if you really wanna learn, then I'm gonna teach you the right way.

Hey Grandpa, is my loop flat ... and is my pivot lookin' good?
   I think I feel everything clickin', just like you said I would.
Hey, see that brockle-face calf with a spot on his rear?
   Watch me plant this honda right between his ears!

Not too fast son … relax … and make sure you're standin' tall,
*   point your finger at your target, and release it like a baseball.*
ATTA BOY … YOU GOT 'ER … and your form wasn't all that bad …
*   Hey, why the long face little buddy … and why do you look so sad?*

Oh, Grandpa, I know I can rope in the corral offa the ground a-course,
    but I wanna be a 'real cowboy' … and rope from offa horse!
You know, like you and Dad, and Uncle Charlie do every day,
    that's the life for me Grandpa, that's the 'cowboy way!'

Listen sprout, I taught your Daddy, and look how he turned out to be,
*   I reckon when all's said and done, he ropes a lot better than me.*
But, there's more to bein' a cowboy than havin' a horse and a rope,
*   So, if you're smart, you'll listen, and then maybe have a little hope.*

You might be little, but you're cowboy, 'cause this ranch belongs to you,
*   make no mistake 'bout it, little pard, you're cowboy through and through.*
So, you get back on that dummy … and throw you a hundred loops a day,
*   and 'fore you know it, son, you'll be cowboy … all the way.*

This theme, "Hey Grandpa," was from the Arizona Cowboy Poets Gathering in Prescott, from 1994. All the poets receive the theme prior to the gathering, and then everyone who wants to, writes a poem around the topic. They then have a session or two with all the poets presenting their poems. The Prescott show is one of our favorites, and certainly one of the best shows on the circuit.

Revelation

I ain't never been too much on politics,
    didn't seem to have the time and such,
    but, I think enough is enough, dear friends,
    for I fear we've all had way too much!

How many of us lost our fathers and brothers,
    fightin' for the symbol of Ol' Glory?
    Well, now they say it's LEGAL to burn that flag ...
    but, that ain't even half the story!

We're in danger of losin' our deeded lands,
    and the right to raise our cattle.
    You better dig in and stock up,
    'cause there's gonna be one helluva battle!

Think you wanna ask God to help,
    'cause it's just the American way?
    You better do it private then,
    for now it ain't legal to publicly pray!

The Hell you say ... we're tough ...
    ain't a battle yet that we ain't won!
    Well, get your head outta the sand ...
    now they're tryin' to take away your gun!

Our damn courts are gridlocked in corruption,
    and miles of red tape.
    They're turnin' loose convicts on the street
    who've committed murder, sodomy and rape!

Somewhere between the ballot box,
    and the stretchin' of the fence line wires,
    our society's breedin' parasites,
    that are dangerous, evil liars!

It ain't foreign aggression anymore,
     you better fear the "New World Order."
     The enemy is right here in your own backyard,
     in the safety of your patriotic borders.

We're takin' in aliens, and boat people,
     so they can breathe freedom's breath?
     Well, we got American citizens in every single state,
     that are already starvin' to death!

You say you want a future,
     that's safe for your son and daughter?
     Well ... don't look now ...
     but we're bein' led like a sheep to slaughter!

We're buildin' our homes on toxic dumps,
     and breathin' murky pollution every day.
     We've become a disposable society,
     that throws everything away!

I'm convinced it ain't politics, friends ...
     it's a matter of religion and much, much more.
     I think it's time we all wake up,
     and realize just who's knockin' at our door!

You see, we've grown lazy and apathetic,
     and we've over-indulged and been enticed.
     It's biblical prophesy come true ...
     the coming of the ANTI-CHRIST!

Read it yourself in the book of Revelation,
     God's word is pure and true,
     but, you better memorize it quickly, friends ...
     before they take your Bible, too!

Tuffy Cooper

It's rare in today's world to measure a man's worth
    by his deeds, and character, and heart.
    For there's not many men that you can read
    who've walked that straight of a path from the start.

But I know one ... cut from the mold of the old days,
    when a man was as good as his word.
    Honor was a handshake, and truth was in his eyes,
    and a cruel remark from his lips was never heard.

He's a rancher ... a father ... a husband ...
    and he epitomizes all that a cowboy should be.
    Gentle in his ways, but tough as nails,
    a perfect living example for all to see.

He's great with kids ... his own, yours or others,
    and as fine a horseman as ever held the reins.
    A cow man, a roper, a mentor to many,
    and a steward of the western plains.

He's history in our midst, his walls are adorned with awards,
    for we've paid tribute to him many times over.
    His house is a trophy case filled with buckles and plaques,
    but inside dwells the soul of an old time drover.

I'm hard pressed for words, but others will agree,
    that they share the same feelings as do I.
    He'll do to ride the river with, and that's hard to find,
    if he's your friend ... it'll be till the day you die.

He's had his wrecks, and durned broke his neck
    more times than some men could ever dream.
    But, he bounces back, like a hot-blooded colt in spring,
    and from the crop he's what we call…"the cream."

I feel I'm a better man for just knowin' him,
    though I don't think I'm worthy to fork his saddle.
    This fella-s already won the war of life,
    while most of us haven't even felt the heat of battle.

He loves his God, and respects his country,
    he's cowboyed hard with grace and style.
    When his trail got rough he hunkered down,
    and gave the world that infectious smile.

Yeah, you're a great cowboy, and a man's man,
    and not so tough that you won't bend,
    but, most of all, I'm proud to say …
    Tuffy Cooper, you're my friend.

I've had the pleasure of knowin' Tuffy for quite a few
years now. I've rode with him, roped with him, bought
horses from him, broke bread with him, and slept under his
roof. He's been the kinda friend that a man is lucky to have
one of in his whole lifetime.

Several years ago, Tuffy booked a show for him and me to do in Carlsbad, New Mexico. Unbeknownst to him, I contacted friends of his from all over the country and many showed up to honor him in a tribute. People from everywhere came to pay homage to this great westerner, and I was not the least bit shocked to see how many people's lives had been touched by him. We presented Tuffy Cooper with the Top Hand Award from the 1st Annual New Mexico Cowboy Classic in 1997. Through all this, he probably treasures my wife's homemade fudge more than any award!

The Epicurean

This homeless fella is camped out in the park,
    and he's feastin' on this big ol' roasted bird.
The Park Ranger spots his smoke and drives up,
    and says, "Howdy stranger, what's the word?"

"Not much," says he, "just campin' for the night,
    then my kids and I are highway bound."
'Bout that time the Ranger, with his watchful eye,
    spots a pile a bald eagle feathers on the ground.

"HEY!" barks the Ranger, "THEM ARE BALD EAGLE FEATHERS!
    Lord, please tell me it ain't so!
That bird you just ate is an endangered species,
    you've just dealt the environment an evil blow!"

"Officer, I'm sorry," says the homeless man,
    'but we ain't ate in a week, maybe two!
I got younguns here that was hungry,
    if you were me … tell me what would you do?"

"I know it's wrong, and I ain't never done it before,
    and I *swear* I'll never do it again.
Please, don't take me to jail, officer …
    these kids ain't got no other kin!"

Well, the Ranger felt real sorry for him,
    and the hoosegow wouldn't help his problems disappear.
He says, "I'm gonna go easy on you this time,
    but, in the mornin' I want you outta here!"

"Oh, thank you sir," says the homeless fella,
   "and in the mornin' we'll be outta here with haste!"
Then curiosity overtook the Ranger, and he says,
   "Tell me … just how does a bald eagle taste?"

"Does it taste like chicken, or turkey,
   or more gamey like water fowl?"
The homeless fella burps his reply,
   "No, it's sorta of a cross between Bar-B-Q Whooping Crane
   and sautéed Spotted Owl!"

Day of Reckoning

I straddle my good gray horse perched on the mesa,
    overlookin' the valley below.
All the years of fond memories tug at my troubles,
    and how tough it'll be to let this place go.

I'm bein' squeezed out by progress, the new age is here,
    but I don't understand what it's all for.
The Environmentalists have swallowed up this ranch,
    with the help of some bureaucratic whore.

Time was, when we ran cattle and harvested wool,
    my ol' daddy stood tall and proud.
But, time marches forward as the death bell rings,
    signaling the finale so loud.

I believe God will show a day, when this whole country realizes
    just who fills their plate.
But, hindsight is as worthless as an unfulfilled dream,
    by then … it'll be too late.

Though sadness dwells in my heart like a flickering light,
    don't shed a tear for me.
For the rancher is a survivor, and stronger than most;
    look inward for the answer, then you'll see.

When the end is upon us, and surely it's due,
    for the scriptures says it's so.
The rancher, in tune with the land, with ear to the ground,
    will hear Gabriel's trumpet blow.

When the line forms up at the Pearly Gates,
　　Sain't Peter will judge just who passes.
He'll say, "Come on in boys, you're welcome here,
　　'cause just like Jesus ... you fed the masses."

Wranglin' Dudes

Several years ago, we decided how to subsidize this ranch,
    and also how to help straighten out some folks' attitudes.
Yep, it was an obvious choice in this day and age,
    so, we took up a-wranglin' dudes.

When they pull up here in their RV's and Beemers,
    I tell 'em, "Just park under that ol' tractor shed.
It ain't been used for a while, like most everything here,
    you see, this ol' place has long since been dead."

They get out and sniff the air, and look around,
    then they ask, "Where's all your cattle?"
I tell 'em, "Oh, the government says we can't raise beef,
    seems we lost the methane gas battle!"

"Well, where's the bunkhouse?" they ask,
    "the corrals, the barn, and the hay baler?"
I tell 'em, "Well, we feed pellets now, don't need a barn,
    and just put your gear in that double-wide trailer."

I'll saddle up some dinks for a five mile loop ride,
    and the dudes are all a-yellin', "Yee Haw, Giddy Up Go!"
I inform them, "Folks, we can't run these horses,
    new rules from the SPCA, don't you know."

We stop for lunch on the trail, and they're really shocked
    when there's no brisket on a sourdough bun.
I explain, "Naw, we ain't had a chuck wagon in years,
    now we eat fast food sandwiches on the run!"

Well, after that little three-hour jaunt,
    they're tuckered out plumb to the bone.
So, I politely point 'em toward the jacuzzi,
    located next to the tennis court and phone.

After their swim, and aerobics class,
    once again they're hungry as a bear.
They seem quite appalled when I light the propane grill,
    but, the EPA says campfires pollute the air!

After supper, they want some hoe-down fun,
    so I tell 'em, "No problem, okeydokey!"
They might be hopin' for a big ol' barn dance,
    but, I can't afford a band, so I give 'em karaoke!

The lights go out in my little dude camp,
    and they're tickled they had a "real" western day.
I'll roust 'em out at the cracka dawn with Egg McMuffins,
    and send 'em on their way.

I charge 'em 500 bucks a day,
    and I sure am glad they pay their bills.
But, little do they know, I got 800 heada
    mother cows, just the other side-a them hills.

I ain't tryin' to con 'em outta their money,
    but, I know they would never understand,
what cowboy life is really like,
    or even appreciate the land.

So, they go home content and happy,
    one day on a ranch sure helps their mood.
Plus, my cows stay calm, and my crew ain't bothered,
    as long as I stay busy wranglin' dudes!

Some Things Never Change

The old timers have told, of days that were old,
    when a puncher dang shore had to hang and rattle.
That breed a-man, always made a top hand,
    'neath the hair of the cinch and the saddle.

Yeah, the horses were rough, but the men were tough,
    and the winters were long, hard and lean.
And you best throw a rope, at a pasture-eatin' lope,
    'cause the cattle were all rank and mean.

Now, one rule of the range, is things always change,
    so, now we're kinda milder and tame.
Maybe the past was okay, but so is today,
    so, let's think how we're alike and the same.

When the snow starts to blow, at twenty below,
    don't we still have to ride and chop ice?
Or, if a calf seems to die, for God only knows why,
    don't the cow and the man both pay the price?

If drought sears the land, as we all know it can,
    don't we still have to haul the elixir of life?
Or, when your whole brandin' crew, consists of just you,
    the younguns, the dog and the wife.

There's no greater pleasure, than God's gift and treasure,
    of a yearlin' colt rompin' in spring.
Who enjoyed it more, us today ... or them before?
    to me, it's 'bout the same thing.

Don't chores still pile up, and dogs still have pups,
don't little boys still wanna be like Dad?
Don't folks bust at the seams, when their kids reach their dreams,
you know, I really don't think that's too bad.

When the market price drops, and shippin' cattle all stops,
don't we each take our belt up and cinch?
It ain't no different today, from what my grandparents say,
than it was for them in a squeeze and a pinch.

Yeah, our horses are bigger, and don't have a hair trigger,
like them snakey ol' broncs that would blow.
And cattle are purebred, and not always grass fed,
like them mossy longhorns of so long ago.

But, a fella still has to make a hand, and ride for the brand,
through winter, spring, summer and fall.
So, near as I can see, between you and me,
there ain't much difference a-tall.

Whether you're a puncher of old, with tales wild and bold,
a rough ridin' rogue of the range.
Or, a modern day man, who's a steward of the land,
out here … some things never change.

Once again, this was a theme topic for the Prescott gathering in 1997. I always enjoy listening to so many poets who take the same title and come up with their own twist on things.

The Old Cocinero

The old cocinero stared into the fire, and sang an old Spanish song
Words that he had sung, since the time that he was young
When he rode the trail north up from Mexico.
He stirred the fire, and the flames leaped higher,
As he felt the cowboy passion and its love;
But the dancin' golden sparks, faded off into the dark,
Disappearin' in the night sky above.

When he rode for the brand, he'd been a top hand,
But now he wrassles pots for the crew.
In his mind he's taken back, to the days of makin' tracks,
With the horses and the men that he knew.
His eyes grew damp, as he looked 'cross the camp,
While he thought 'bout compadres now long gone
In their prime they'd won the battle, snappin' broncs and cuttin' cattle;
Now their range is taken over by their sons.

His tired bones are achin', and he knows the West is changin',
But he wonders why things have to move so fast.
Then a dream of silver bridles, comes shining through the shadows,
Like glowin' embers buried in the ash,
Like a Spanish song he's sung, since the time that he was young,
When he rode trail north up from Mexico.

The changin' of the guard was a blow that stuck him hard,
They've forgotten who he was and what he did.
After all the risks he took, he's just an ol' camp cook,
Ridin' nighthawk on a cavvey fulla kids.
You tie your knots, in the end that's all you've got,
And these boys will tie theirs hard and fast and true;
And Lord they're brave and bold, like vaqueros of old,
Who rode the trails back when the West was new.

Like raindrops without number, the shooting stars of summer,
Are the good luck that the new day will bring.
In the hours before sunrise, cuttin' apples for the days pies,
He leans against the wagon box and sings
A Spanish song he's sung, since the time that he was young,
When he rode the trail north up from Mexico.

Kerry Grombacher and I co-wrote this as a song for my "Chase The Wind" album, but it has such a great sentiment, we felt it would go nicely in this volume of works.

Rancho Chorro Grande

Sing me a song, ol' Sespe River,
    whistlin' winds sweeten my ear;
High on the mountain, follow the condor,
    the valley below beckons me here.

A white palomino, stands ol' "Sundance,"
    stronger than most and runs like the wind.
He carries me through ol' Chorro Grande,
    ridin' the trails back home again.

Scrub oak growin' wild on the hillside,
    high desert air plays with the sun.
Come late November, first snow of the season,
    a warm fire's glowin' till winter is done.

Gone am I to ol' Chorro Grande
    to play with the eagle and reach for the sky;
My spirit will fly on ol' Chorro Grande
    on a stud I call "Sundance," ridin' so high.

Me and Pardner Hicks on "Sundance" and "Bandit"
    sharin' the land with beaver and pine.
When Frank D. Felt wrote "Songs Of The Sespe"
    he left blank a page I feel that is mine.

Chaparral race with deer and coyote;
    each try to live to see the next day.
A blizzard of stars blanket the heaven;
    shadowing a night the sun takes away.

High on the mesa above Wheeler Hot Springs
    ride only rancheros with love for the land.
Look for me there when my life is over
    buried 'neath cedar with God near my hand.

❧ ❦

    My time at Rancho Chorro Grande from 1985-1987 was a turning point in my life. Famed western author, Frank D. Felt, homesteaded the place and his original cabin was converted into the ranch headquarters. Banditos hid out in the area as late as the 1920's 'cause the area is so remote and rugged. The last of the American condors roost there, nestled in mountains that have cave pain'tings from the Chumash Indians. It is truly a magical place, an American treasure, and a gift from God.

Goin' Back Home

I'm splittin' the cool night air on the highway,
tryin' to figger out where I went wrong.
Why in Sam Hell did I ever leave her?
She never did nothin' but make me strong.

Maybe, I was too young and wild,
or maybe, I was just too blind to see.
But, hindsight's got 20/20 vision,
now it's clear what she meant to me.

Starin' at miles of white lines,
my mind starts to stray, and I wonder,
am I a victim of poor judgment,
like some little school boy's blunder?

She always took care of me,
and God knows my family was in her heart.
I feel like a damn fool,
for even thinkin' I should depart.

I know if she's still there,
I'll stay with her forever,
and if she only will take me back,
to leave her ... I would never.

I've always deeply loved her,
and that feelin' has never died.
She gave me a sense of belonging,
from her strength of southern pride.

I've defended her with honor,
and her shortcomings I've overcame.
I put one man on is backside,
just for tryin' to besmirch her good name.

Somehow, I think she'll understand,
I was a rogue who had to stray.
Perhaps, she'll think what's most important,
is that I'm returning to her today.

The sun is brightly climbin',
and I feel it's gonna be a good day.
I hope her mood is forgiving,
'cause I've seen the err of my way.

There she is, her arms are open wide,
and no more shall I have to roam,
hello my love ... TEXAS ...
it sure is good to be home.

I spent the first 30 years of my life in Texas, so it'll always have a special place in my heart. After my grandparents had passed on, we sold the family holdings, closed the door on that chapter, and moved on. Even though New Mexico has been my home for some years now, I'll forever treasure the roots I have in the hill country of "God's country."

A Cowboy Prayer

I thank you, Lord, for all that you've given me,
　　my life is truly rich through Your divinity.

I'm a little hard-pressed for the right words to say,
　　but, You know what's in my heart, Lord, with each passing day.

I know when it's stormy, and there's rain on my trail,
　　it's just Your way of showin' me that You shall prevail.

I just figger that You are the only one to really trust,
　　'cause I know that, eventually, I'll return to dust.

So, while You got me here, Lord, I'll enjoy Your earthly treasure,
　　and I'll do my best to match up to your standard of measure.

Do what You will with me, Lord, and I'll try not to stumble,
　　let me be kind to others, and please help me stay humble.

I thank you, Lord, for the blessings that You put here before me,
　　and bless You, Father, for the strength of spirit to restore Thee.

Please watch over my family, loved ones, and friends,
　　and guide us all safely to where Your Heaven's gate begins.

Alphabetical Index of Poems

Order Form

☐ Yes! Please send me the following merchandise.

Name_____

Address_____

City_____ State_____ Zip_____

Phone_____Fax_____

Title	Qty.	Each	Total
Cowboy Poetry, Contemporary Verse 47 original cowboy poems from Duke Davis Illustrated by Ron Kil	_____	$20.00	_____
Audio Tapes and CDs by Duke Davis			
Blue Texas Sky, contemporary cowboy swing music by Duke Davis CD—$15; Cassette—$10	_____	$	_____
Follow the Wagon, traditional cowboy music from Duke Davis CD—$15; Cassette—$10	_____	$	_____
Chase the Wind, original cowboy music by Duke Davis, CD—$15; Cassette—$10	_____	$	_____
All Points West, original cowboy poetry by Duke Davis (Cassette only)	_____	$10.00	_____
Time to Ride, two album set of original cowboy music and poetry with traditional Western music (Cassette only)	_____	$10.00	_____
	Subtotal		_____
Please add $3.00 for the first item, plus $1.00 for each additional item for shipping and handling.	**S&H**		_____
Foreign orders must be accompanied by a postal money order in U.S. funds.	**TOTAL**		_____

Send check or money order to: Rockin' Double "D" Productions
1919 Fifth Street, Suite O, Santa Fe, NM 87505
To order by phone call (505) 474-9238. Fax: (505) 474-9241.
E-Mail: duke@rockindd.com Website: www.rockindd.com